The Future
of
History

Howard Zinn

Interviews with
David Barsamian

Common Courage Press   Monroe, Maine

Library of Congress Cataloging-in-Publication Data
CIP

Zinn, Howard, 1922-
    The future of history : interviews with David Barsamian /
Howard Zinn.
        p. cm.
    Includes index.
    ISBN 1-56751-157-0. -- ISBN 1-56751-156-2 (pbk.)
    1. History, Modern--Philosophy. 2. Zinn, Howard, 1922-
--Interviews. 3. Historians--United States--Interviews.
I. Barsamian, David. II. Title.
D16.9Z56 1999
901--dc21
                                                    98-54696
                                                        CIP

Common Courage Press
P.O. Box 702
Monroe ME 04951

www.commoncouragepress.com

207-525-0900
Fax: 207-525-3068

First Printing

Contents

CONTENTS

Introduction

"I hate introductions," Howard Zinn said to me most emphatically. Honoring his wishes I'll cut to the quick. The interviews were recorded for broadcast. The text retains much of the conversational style. Some humor is lost in transcription but I hope enough survives to give you a chuckle or two. The first two interviews were done at KGNU in Boulder, Colorado. We did the LaGuardia one at Hampshire College in Amherst. All the others were recorded at the Harvard Trade Union Program office which occasionally serves as Alternative Radio's Boston-area studio. Interview excerpts have appeared in *The Progressive* and Z. It is inspiring to work with a mensch like Howard Zinn, even if he does like the coffee at Dunkin' Donuts!

Reflections on History

October 25, 1989

DB *What about the notion of history as a commodity, something that can be bought and sold. Do you accept that?*

I once wrote an essay called "History as Private Enterprise." What I meant was that I thought so much history was written without a social conscience behind it. Or if there was a social conscience somewhere in the historian, it was put aside for the writing of history, because writing history was done as a professional duty. It was done to get something published, to get a job at a university, to get tenure, to get a promotion, to build up one's prestige. It was printed by publishers in books that would sell and make a profit. The profit motive has so distorted our whole economic and social system by making profit the key to what is produced and therefore leaving important things unproduced while producing stupid things, and leaving some people rich and some people poor. That same profit system had extended to that world of academic institutions, which as an innocent young student I thought was a world separated from the world of commerce and business. But the world of the university, of publishing, of history, of scholarship is not at all separated from the profit-seeking world. The historian doesn't think of it consciously this way. But there is the fact of economic security that operates in every profession. The professional writer and historian is perhaps conscious, perhaps semi-conscious, or perhaps has already absorbed into the bloodstream a thinking about economic security and therefore about playing it safe. You don't have to conspire to have bad history, inadequate history, history from the top down. All you have to do is play it safe, and that's the rule. I guess it's the American rule, generally, for professionals. Play it safe. And so historians, most of them, play it safe. And the textbook publishers help in that. The textbook publishers want to play it safe. They don't want to say anything which might raise an eyebrow anywhere. The same is true of heads of departments and administrators at colleges and universities. So we get a lot of safe history.

DB *Who are the custodians of history in terms of gender, class, race, and ideology?*

They are mostly guys, mostly well off, mostly white. Sometimes this is talked about as the history of rich, white men. There's a history which is done by rich white men. Not that historians are rich. But the people who publish the textbooks are, the people who control the media, the people who decide what historians to invite on the networks at special moments when they want to call on a historian. The people who dominate the big media networks are rich. Not only are those who control our information rich, white and male, but they then ask that history concentrate on those who are rich, white and male. That is why the point of view of black people has not been a very important one in the telling of our history. The point of view of women certainly has not been. The point of view of working people is something that has not been given its due in the histories that we have mostly been given in our culture.

Jesse Lemisch, a dissident historian, calls them the "great white fathers" of history. I guess that's generally true. I don't want to be too harsh with these guardians, because it's not a matter of single individuals. It's a sort of general atmosphere that pervades the historical profession which is dominated by that word: "safety." And then there are others like Staughton Lynd, for instance, who is a remarkable historian. He taught with me. I don't say he's a remarkable historian just because he taught with me. We were colleagues at Spelman College in Atlanta. A wonderful person. His parents were distinguished academics, Helen and Robert Lynd who wrote *Middletown*. He came up in this rarefied academic setting, but he was a radical from the time he was, like, two.

After he left Spelman College he went to Yale. He was a prize-winning scholar. But then in 1965, we had just started bombing, at least officially, Vietnam. He flew to Hanoi. Came back and suddenly he was *persona non grata* at Yale. Didn't get tenure. Left Yale. Tried to get another job. You'd think somebody who'd taught at Yale is not going to have trouble getting another job. He couldn't get another teaching job anywhere in the country. This was past the period of McCarthyism. They always make this mistake. They think McCarthyism occupied a finite period in American history. McCarthyism is a permanent fact of American life. I can tell you exactly how it works about safety. At one point when Lynd was having trouble getting a job I said to a colleague of mine who was a big shot in the history department at Boston University, I hear you're looking for somebody to teach American history. He said, Yeah. I said, How about Staughton Lynd. He said, Staughton Lynd? I said, You know him? He said, I was on his doctoral committee at Columbia. I said, What do you think of him? He said, Brilliant. I said, Well, how about it? He said, Oh, we could never do that. I said, Why? He said, Well, of course, I'd like him. But then he would never be approved. And that's the way it works. It's like, I would love to have black people on my block, but my neighbors wouldn't like it.

DB *Let's talk a bit about historical engineering, since you are a historian.*

And since I'm an engineer.

DB *You may have some engineering inclinations. Certainly there's been a lot of engineering around the U.S. wars in Indochina. I think the way I'm phrasing the question is already tipping off something I want to get in there, and that is, it's always referred to as the Vietnam War, whereas Laos and Cambodia were sideshows and never discussed. What kind of engineering have you seen evolve in the last twenty or twenty-five years around Indochina?*

A lot of it is not engineering but, what's the word they use when they raze cities? What do you do when you raze history?

DB *Obliteration.*

Sort of leaving it out. You look at the newest textbooks and you see two paragraphs on Vietnam. What's going on here? It's the central event of our generation in the U.S. Where is it? So that's one thing that goes on. The other thing that goes on is, when they talk about it in the popular press especially, the tone is, Well, we didn't do it right. It's a tactical question. We could have won. Part of it is there are a lot of books out now by military specialists about how we might have won. We didn't do enough. As I've often commented, we only dropped seven million tons of bombs on 35 million people. We didn't do enough. The other is, there's a sort of subtle thing that's happened in connection with Vietnam veterans. You've noticed the last three, four or five years with the Vietnam Memorial, there's been much more attention now to Vietnam and Vietnam veterans. But the mood of it all is dominated by, We haven't done enough for the veterans. Which is true, of course, because you never do enough for the veterans. But underlying that, and connected with that, is a romanticization of the war that the veterans fought. It's sort of carried along with a legitimate sympathy for the veterans. Along with a legitimate sympathy for the veterans there's a hitchhiking idea, which is that, You know, the war they fought was noble in some way. They tried their best. It didn't work out. People are afraid to confront the ugliness and immorality of the war, although there are Vietnam veterans that confront it.

That's another thing that's ignored, the writings and the thoughts of so many Vietnam veterans who hate the war, hate their part in it, hate what the U.S. did in Southeast Asia. There's a whole bunch of people like that. There's an organization called Veterans for Peace. Is it known at all? Maybe not. But they consist of veterans of the Vietnam War and other wars. That makes me eligible. Veterans who repudiate war. There's an outfit in New England called the Smedley Butler Brigade. Have you ever heard of that?

DB *The Marine Corps general.*

The Marine Corps general who later on turned into a real whistleblower. Imagine a whistleblower in the Marines. Blowing the whistle on the Marines is not an easy task. You're taking your life in your hands. Butler said, I was a hired thug for Wall Street, for all the great corporations. We went into Nicaragua, Honduras, and we did it for the great corporations. The Smedley Butler Brigade is a group of veterans who are opposed to American policy in Central America and elsewhere. The media don't pay any attention to them. The media don't pay attention to the Vietnam veterans who take a proper angry attitude towards the Vietnam War. So that's part of the process of engineering, I think, that you're talking about.

DB *We had the interesting spectacle, and it's absolutely staggering, in fact, of the Soviet Foreign Minister calling the Soviet invasion of Afghanistan "illegal and immoral." Might there come a day when an*

American Secretary of State might describe the U.S. invasion of Grenada or the bombing of Libya or the intervention in Indochina in those terms?

Isn't that interesting? Here's the U.S., the free society, and here's the Soviet Union, the totalitarian society. They're both imperial powers. They've both done these terrible things to other countries, and the country that comes forward first to confess its sins is the Soviet Union. They make us look sick. Gorbachev is making Bush look sick. Will there come a time? Maybe. If there's an American movement strong enough, and if the U.S. gets embarrassed enough by what happens in the rest of the world. If the pressures around the rest of the world become...

DB   *What about a glasnost within the U.S. What are the historical precedents and possibilities for that?*

Precedents for *glasnost*? Was there ever a period when a hundred flowers bloomed in the U.S.? No, only in *Better Homes and Gardens*, but not in thought. There are no precedents except the precedents that people created when dissidents and radicals forced their ideas through all these blockades to get the attention of millions of people in certain periods of American history. This was done in the antislavery movement. William Lloyd Garrison's *Liberator* started off with twelve subscribers and ended up with 100,000 people reading it. Or during the Populist movement, when the Populists had millions of people reading their pamphlets all over the country. The Socialist Party. Their papers had a circulation of several million. *Appeal to Reason* was read by a million people. There were periods in American history when dissident movements fighting uphill against the control of opinion got to the attention of lots of people. During the Vietnam War and during the civil rights movement there was that kind of a breakthrough. So there are those kinds of precedents. I can see the possibility. But not *glasnost*, not from the top. The Soviet Union, and maybe this more conforms to its history, had a *glasnost* from the top. Although I don't doubt that it was a response to the currents swirling below in the Soviet Union, which we didn't see easily. In the U.S. I think that *glasnost* is most likely to come as a result of a great social movement down below.

DB   *In talking about the steady decline in voting in the U.S., you've said that it's a sign of the "increased sophistication of the American* *electorate." I'm wondering if it's not so much sophistication as just genuine cynicism.*

I was just having a little fun with "sophistication." I agree. It's cynicism. It's pessimism. It's disgust. It's fatigue at having to choose between one mediocrity and another every four years. I call it sophistication not because it's born of a deep consciousness about the American political system. It's sophisticated in the sense that it recognizes that the two-party system as the American political system operates is inadequate to represent the interests and needs of the American people. In that sense it's sophisticated.

DB *You've seen the evolution of the American labor movement. It was once in the vanguard of progressive movements in the U.S. Today you have the specter of blue-collar workers wearing T-shirts saying "Union-free and Proud." What do you attribute that to?*

It's a sad story what's happened to the American labor movement, if you trace it from the IWW especially through the CIO and down to the present day. The labor movement is a victim of the general American culture and the lack of a very strong radical movement in the U.S. It leaves the working people of the U.S. absolutely prone before CBS and NBC and the 6 o'clock news and the glimmers of stuff that get in newspapers. The American mainstream culture is so barren and so poor that when Reagan broke the air controllers' strike, nobody was speaking out against it, nobody was saying to workers all across the country, Don't you recognize? This is you tomorrow. It's not just the air controllers. So it's part of the general decline of social consciousness in American culture.

But I would point to something that I think we shouldn't overlook. At the top of the labor movement there were all these corrupt and ignorant and conservative people, including agents of the FBI.

DB *Jackie Pressler of the Teamsters Union*

And all of that. There is a labor movement which is not in those high circles of money and corruption, which exists all over on a scale that's not very noticed in the press and unfortunately not even noticed by people around the country themselves. I'm talking about the fact that there's a lot of new white-collar organizing, a lot of

organizing of secretaries and technical workers and non-skilled workers which is taking place and which still has a kind of grass-roots
enthusiasm that the old unions used to have in the 1930s when the
CIO was coming up. But it doesn't have the look of a national movement. In the U.S., unless something becomes national it isn't noticed.
There's something about the way the country operates and the way
the media control things that local things remain local. Local news
remains local. So if the clerical workers at Harvard win a wonderful
strike against the University and finally succeed in unionizing this bas-
tion of anti-unionism, hardly anybody in the country knows about it.

DB *This goes to what you have said in the past about a lot of the
news not getting reported. Simply omitted.*

It's like history. News is just a contemporary version of history,
and journalists are contemporary versions of what historians are.
Yesterday is history.

DB *I'm still interested in this decline of the American labor movement. Erwin Knoll, the editor of* The Progressive, *suggested it was
McCarthyism and the witch-hunting of the 1940s and 1950s that really
smashed the left core of the unions. Does that make any sense to you?*

I'm dubious about that. It's too easy an explanation. Repression
has an effect. There's no question about that. And the government did
work to smash the IWW and smash the Socialist Party and
McCarthyism did take its toll. But I don't think repression is enough if
other conditions are right. That is, during the Vietnam War, let's put
it this way, the FBI worked hard to repress the movement. The
COINTELPRO was a vast operation. It lasted for fifteen years and was
designed to cripple the New Left. They did not succeed, because the
fact of the war and how that war came across to people was too powerful for that movement to be repressed. They couldn't do it to the civil
rights movement, either. The only reason repression worked against
the Black Panthers was not because of the repression itself but because
the movement was not capable of dealing with the post-segregation
situation of black people with the very deep problems, class problems,
of black people and the economic structure of the country. The movement was not capable of doing that. Yes, the FBI did its job and killed
people and the Panthers were crushed. But that wasn't it. So I never

think that repression is enough. I think that if other circumstances are right, movements can defy repression.

DB   *During the Reagan Administration there was a thrust on "bedroom issues": who you slept with, what you said, what people could say on the radio, in art and in books and the whole abortion issue. What do you attribute this sudden interest and attention to lifestyle issues to?*

Again, is this a conspiracy? But however it started, certainly it's a neat way of diverting people's attention from the important social issues which exist at a time when there's no national movement powerful enough to overcome that. After all, those private things and those bedroom items always exist. It's just that sometimes they're paid attention and other times they're not. They're paid attention to, I think, when there isn't enough going on in the culture and they can rise to the top. At other times I think they are overwhelmed. There are times when history itself, the events are so powerful that they overwhelm those peripheral items. We obviously haven't reached that point yet.

DB   *Along with the attention that's given to those issues is an enormous growth in the poor and the homeless. Ted Kennedy used to joke that Reagan liked the poor so much he was creating millions and millions of them. So there you had a sort of parallel development that wasn't quite getting the attention of Senators and Congressmen. What do you make of it?*

It has to do with voting, and who votes. The poor don't vote. The people who are concerned with these lifestyle and private issues are the people who go to the polls more. The homeless certainly don't go to the polls. When you look at the fifty percent of the people who don't vote in presidential elections, most of them are poor. So it's a very common thing in American politics that you can ignore the poor. You can't ignore the middle class. You can't ignore the upper class, but you can ignore the poor.

DB   *Finally, I'd like to ask about your involvement in World War II as a bombardier. Studs Terkel has called that the "good war," the war against Hitler, Mussolini and Tojo.*

He puts it in quotation marks, though. The "good war."

DB   *Would there be any instance where you would advocate the use of force?*

When I participated in World War II, more than participated in the sense that I volunteered. I was enthusiastic, I was a gung-ho eager bombardier. I guess I believed at that time in the idea of just wars and unjust wars, and that was a just war. Then after the war I moved away from that. I came to the conclusion, looking at the results of World War II, the forty million dead and the two superpowers armed with enough to destroy the world, that there could be no such thing as a just war any more. There's no ideological reason, no territorial reason, no reason that can justify the cruelty of war. The means of war have reached the point where they overwhelm any possible decent ends. I had a student of mine once write something in her journal. My students kept journals based on what we were talking about in class and giving their reactions. The student said, They're always classifying wars like they classify wines. This was a good year. This was a bad year. This was a good war. This was a bad war. I say, Wars are not like wine. War is like cyanide. One drop and you're dead.

One Step Ahead of the Landlord

November 11, 1992

DB *Tell me something about your roots.*

I was born in 1922. I grew up in a working class family in the slums of Brooklyn. My parents met as factory workers in New York. They were Jewish immigrants. My father came from Austria, my mother from Asiatic Russia, Siberia. I remember moving and changing schools all the time. We were always one step ahead of the landlord. My father struggled. He went from job to job. I always wanted to get out of the house. Where we lived was never a nice place to be. So I was in the streets a lot. I understand what it's like for kids to live in and prefer the streets. That's how I grew up.

When I got to be college age I went to work in a shipyard and became a shipyard worker for three years. My family needed the money. I volunteered for the Air Force and was a bombardier. I got married before I went overseas. After the war my wife and I first lived in Bedford-Stuyvesant in a rat-infested basement. I'm building up my sordid past, trying to evoke tears. We were so happy when we were accepted into the Lillian Wald low-income housing project on the east side of New York. We lived there for seven years while I went to NYU under the GI bill and to graduate school at Columbia. My wife worked. Our two kids were in nursery school.

DB *What was the language at home when you were growing up? Did you speak Yiddish?*

Not me. My parents spoke Yiddish to each other, so I understood it. When they spoke to us they spoke English, nicely accented, with a few Yiddish words thrown in. I never actually used Yiddish, but I still can understand it. Words like "bagel" and "knish."

DB *Your father was a waiter for many years. He'd work a bar mitzvah and then there'd be no work.*

He did a lot of Jewish weddings. In fact, when I was about seventeen he introduced me to it. On New Year's Eve they would be short and the waiters would be able to bring their sons in. They called them "juniors." It was an AFL craft union. Everything was hereditary: the leadership of the union, the jobs, etc. I really hated being a waiter, and I felt for my father. They used to call him "Charlie Chaplin" because he walked like Chaplin. His feet were flat. They said it was the result of all those years of being a waiter. I don't know if that's true or not, but that was the story. He worked very hard. He, and a lot of others like him, was a great fan of Roosevelt during the New Deal. People were still getting married, but they weren't paying waiters. My father worked a variety of jobs, as a window cleaner, a pushcart peddler and a ditch digger with the WPA. My mother had been a factory worker before she was married. When she got married she began having kids, and it was my father's job to support the family.

DB *Was there any kind of intellectual life at home, books, magazines?*

There were no books or magazines. The very first book I read I picked up on the street. Ten pages were ripped out, but it didn't matter to me because it was my first book. I was already reading, and this was *Tarzan and the Jewels of Opar*. I'll always remember that. No books at home. However, my parents knew that I liked books and liked to read, and then the *New York Post* came out with this gift, that if you clipped these coupons and sent in twenty five cents, they would send you a volume of Dickens. So my parents sent away for the whole set of Dickens, the collected works, twenty volumes. I read every single one. Dickens was my first author. Some of them I didn't understand, like *The Pickwick Papers*. Sometimes I got the humor and sometimes I didn't. I went through them in order. I thought if the *New York Post* sent you the books in order, somehow they must have a reason for it. So first it was *David Copperfield*, then *Oliver Twist*, then *Dombey and Son*, then *Bleak House*. When I was thirteen my parents bought me a typewriter. They didn't know about typewriters or books, but they knew I was interested in reading and writing. They paid five dollars for a remade Underwood No. 5, which I had for a very long time.

DB *Looking at the politics of history, you're fond of quoting Orwell's dictum "Who controls the past controls the future. Who controls the present controls the past."*

Orwell is one of my favorite writers. When I came across that I knew I had to use it. We writers are real thieves. We see something good and use it, and then if we're nice we say where we got it. Sometimes we don't. What the Orwell quote means to me is a very important observation that if you can control history, what people know about it, if you can decide what's in people's history and what's left out, you can order their thinking. You can order their values. You can in effect organize their brains by controlling their knowledge. The people who can do that, who can control the past, are the people who control the present. The people who would dominate the media, who publish the textbooks, who decide in our culture what are the dominant ideas, what gets told and what doesn't.

DB *You've said that objectivity and scholarship in the media and elsewhere is not only "harmful and misleading, it's not desirable."*

I've said two things about it. One, that it's not possible. Two, it's not desirable. It's not possible because all history is a selection out of an infinite number of facts. As soon as you begin to select, you select according to what you think is important. Therefore it is already not objective. It's already biased in the direction of whatever you, as the selector of this information, think people should know. So it's really not possible. Of course, some people claim to be objective. The worst thing is to claim to be objective. Of course you can't be. Historians should say what their values are, what they care about, what their background is, and let you know what is important to them so that young people and everybody who reads history are warned in advance that they should never count on any one source, but should go to many sources. So it's not possible to be objective, and it's not desirable if it were possible. We should have history that does reflect points of view and values, in other words, history that is not objective. We should have history that enhances human values, humane values, values of brotherhood, sisterhood, peace, justice and equality. The closest I can get to it is the values enunciated in the Declaration of Independence. Equality, the right of all people to have life, liberty and the pursuit of happiness. Those are values that historians should actively promulgate in writing history. In doing that they needn't distort or omit important things. But it does mean if they have those values in mind, that they will emphasize those things in history which will bring up a new generation of people who read history books and who will care about treating other people equally, about doing away with war, about justice in every form.

DB *How do you filter those biases?*

As I've said, yes, I have my biases, my leanings. So if I'm writing or speaking about Columbus, I will try not to hide or omit the fact that Columbus did a remarkable thing in crossing the ocean and venturing out into uncharted waters. It took physical courage and navigational skill. It was a remarkable event. I have to say that so that I don't omit what people see as the positive side of Columbus. But then I have to go on to say the other things about Columbus which are much more important than his navigational skill or that he was a religious man. That is how he treated the human beings that he found in this hemisphere. The enslavement, the torture, the murder, the dehumanization of these people. That is the important thing.

There's an interesting way in which you can frame a sentence which will show what you emphasize and which will have two very different results. Here's what I mean. Take Columbus as an example. You can frame it, and this was the way the Harvard historian Samuel Eliot Morison in effect framed it in his biography of Columbus: Columbus committed genocide, but he was a wonderful sailor. He did a remarkable and extraordinary thing in finding these islands in the Western Hemisphere. Where's the emphasis there? He committed genocide, but...He's a good sailor. I say, He was a good sailor, but he treated people with the most horrible cruelty. Those are two different ways of saying the same facts. Depending on which side of the comma you're on, you show your bias. I believe that it's good for us to put our biases in the direction of a humane view of history.

DB *I know you were present at the 1892 celebration of the four hundredth anniversary of Columbus' voyage...*

Of course, I try to be at all these important events. I tried to be there in 1492 but I didn't make it.

DB *In terms of 1992, were you surprised at the level of protest, indignation and general criticism of Columbus?*

I was delightfully surprised. I did expect more protest this year than there ever has been, because I knew, just from going around the country speaking and from reactions to my book [*A People's History of the United States*], which has sold a couple of hundred thousand copies. It starts off with Columbus. So anybody who has read it I hope is going to have a different view of him. I knew that there has been more literature in the last few years. Hans Koenig's wonderful book, which appeared before mine, *Columbus' Enterprise*. I was aware that Native American groups around the country were planning protests. So I knew that things would happen, but I really wasn't prepared for the number of things that have happened and the extent of protest that there has been. It has been very satisfying. What's interesting about it, much as people like me and you rail against the media, they don't have total control. It is possible for us, and this is very heartwarming and encouraging, even though we don't control the major media, by sheer word of mouth, a little radio broadcast, community newspapers, speaking here and there, Noam Chomsky speaking seventeen times a day in a hundred cities, to actually change the culture in a very important way. And it does happen. For example, the *New York Times* reported that this year the Columbus quincentennial is marked by protests. In Denver they called off a parade because of the expected protest. This has happened in a number of other places. Berkeley changed Columbus Day to Indigenous Peoples Day.

DB *So there is in this doom and gloom atmosphere that the left loves to wash itself in at times glimpses of light?*

I am encouraged by what I see. Not just about Columbus, but that as soon as you give people information that they didn't have before, they are ready to accept it. When I went around the country speaking, I was worried that when I started describing the atrocities that Columbus committed, that people in the audience would start yelling and shouting and throwing things at me, threatening my life. That hasn't happened at all. Maybe the worst that happened is that one Italian-American said to me in a low voice, plaintively, "What are Italians going to do? Who are we going to celebrate?" I said, "Joe

DiMaggio, Arturo Toscanini, Pavoratti, Fiorello LaGuardia, a whole bunch of wonderful Italians that we can celebrate."

It's been very encouraging. I believe that all over this country there are people who really want change. I don't mean the minuscule change that Clinton represents. I suppose a minuscule change is better than the no change that we've been having. But there are people who want much more change than the parties are offering.

DB *Are you encouraged also by the development of new media, community radio stations, cable TV, Z magazine, Common Courage Press, South End Press and the Open Magazine pamphlet series?*

Oh, yes.

DB *Is there anything in American history that parallels this burst of independent media in the last ten or fifteen years?*

There have been periods when pamphlets and newspapers have had an important effect in arousing and organizing a movement. In the years leading up to the Revolutionary War there was a lot of pamphleteering that was not under the control of the colonial governors. In the time of the antislavery movement, the Abolitionists spread literature all over the country, so much so that Andrew Jackson ordered the Postmaster General to bar abolitionist literature from the Southern states. That's Andrew Jackson, our great hero. We've had labor newspapers. The populist movement put out an enormous number of pamphlets. But in this era of television and radio, where they soon became dominated by these monster, fabulously wealthy networks crowding critical voices off the air, it's been very refreshing just in the past few years to see these new media. I could see this in the Gulf War. I was invited to a gathering of several hundred community broadcasters in Cambridge. I didn't know so many existed. During the Gulf War they were about the only place where you could hear Noam Chomsky and other people who would give you an analysis of the war in a critical way. You weren't getting that on public television and radio, certainly not on the major media. Now there are satellite dishes. It's amazing that people in the progressive movement are able to use these satellite dishes to beam broadcasts all over. Wherever I go there are community newspapers. That's what we have to depend on, and we should make the most of it.

DB *In the popular culture, ideology and propaganda are attributes of our adversaries. It's not something that we have here in our democracy. How do you persuade people that in fact there is a good deal of propaganda and a great amount of ideology right here in the United States?*

The best way I can persuade them that what we get mostly from the media and the textbooks and the histories is ideological, biased not in the humanist direction but towards wealth and power, expansion, militarism and conquest, is to give them examples from history and to show how the government has manipulated our information. You can go back to the Spanish-American War and talk about how the history textbooks all said that the reason we got into that war was that popular opinion demanded it. Therefore the President went along. There were no public opinion polls then, no mass rallies on behalf of going into Cuba. By public opinion they meant a few powerful newspapers. So when I get to the Vietnam War I talk about how the government manipulated the information, not only the general public, but the newspapers, and Congress. They fabricated incidents in the Gulf of Tonkin in the summer of 1964 to give Lyndon Johnson an excuse to go before Congress and get them to pass a resolution giving him carte blanche to start the war full-scale. I talk about the history books and how they omit what the United States has done in Latin America, and how when they get to the Spanish-American War they will talk about what we did in Cuba but not much about what we did in the Philippines. The war in Cuba lasted three months, while the war in the Philippines lasted for years. It was a big, bloody, Vietnam-type war. So I try to give historical examples to show how that ideology manifests itself.

DB *Speaking of the Vietnam War, it seems it will never end. We saw examples of that in the 1992 Presidential campaign, with questions about draft status, who fought and who didn't, and the ongoing MIA/POW issue. Why is that? Why does it persist?*

The administrations, the powers that be, the people who got us into the Vietnam War and kept us in it, didn't like the way it ended. They're trying to change the ending, to rewrite history. They're saying: the reason we lost is because of the media and the antiwar movement. Or we fought with one hand behind our back. We dropped seven million tons of bombs, twice as much as we dropped in World

War II, and they claim that was "one hand tied behind our back." Incredible. They were very unhappy not just that we lost the war, but about what happened in the war, the carnage that people became aware of. The My Lai massacre. The destruction of the Vietnamese countryside. The deaths of a million people in Vietnam and of 55,000 Americans. They worry that those events made the American people leery of military intervention. All the surveys taken after the Vietnam War in the late 1970s showed that the American people did not want military intervention anywhere in the world, for any reason. The military industrial political establishment has been trying desperately to change that view and to try to get the American people to accept military intervention as once more the basic American policy. Grenada was a probe, Panama another, the war in the Middle East a bigger one.

DB *They were all short and fast.*

Exactly. They learned a number of things from Vietnam. If you're going to have a war, do it quickly. Don't give the public a chance to know what's happening. Control the information, so the war will be over before anybody really knows the truth about what happened. Here it is now, a year or two later, and only now we're finding out that the Bush Administration was arming Saddam Hussein right up to just before the war. So keep the war short. And try to have very few casualties, and don't mention the casualties on the other side. Then you can call it a "costless war." Even if 100,000 Iraqis die, even if tens of thousands of children die in Iraq, they don't count as people. So you can say it was an easy war.

DB *You're fond also of quoting Chomsky and Edward Herman in* Manufacturing Consent. *They observe that it's hard to make a case about the manipulation of the media when they find that they're so willing to go along.*

I like that quote because so many people fall in with the media when the media say the government is controlling the information, and want desperately to tell the truth to the public. But of course they don't. In the Iraqi war they showed themselves to be such weak, pathetic, absolutely obsequious yea-sayers to the briefers in Washington. They kept putting generals and ex-Joint Chiefs of Staff personnel on the air, military experts, to make us all exult in the smart bombs that were being dropped. The media did not put anybody who would give any historical background, or who would criticize the war on the air.

DB *One of your intellectual favorites is Alan Dershowitz.*

Sure [chuckles].

DB *In a recent column he was writing about the atrocities in the Balkans and decrying the use of the Nazi analogy. He says it is "overused and automatically invoked and as a result nearly bereft of cognitive content." What do you think of that?*

Analogies have to be used carefully. They can be misused. Sometimes they are not used as analogies but as identities. If you say something is like something, people will say, Oh, you're saying it *is* that. It is possible to overuse the Nazi analogy until it loses its force. I was speaking to a group of high school students in Boston the other day. One of them asked, Who was worse, Hitler or Columbus? There's a nice analogy. They are two different situations, two different forms of genocide. In fact, in that situation it was not an exaggeration. In terms of the numbers of people who died, the Hitler killing was smaller than the number of people who died in the genocide not committed directly by Columbus, but as a result of the work of the *conquistadores*, including Columbus and the others. When they got through with the Caribbean and Latin America, perhaps fifty million indigenous people or more died as a result of enslavement, overwork, direct execution and disease. A much higher toll even than the genocide of Hitler.

I think it's all right to invoke analogies, so long as you invoke them carefully and make the differences and the similarities clear.

DB *In addition to wiping out the indigenous population, the Europeans had to initiate the slave trade and bring over Africans to work the land.*

When the Indians were gone as workers, that's when the slave trade began, and another genocide took place, tens of millions of black slaves brought over, dying by the millions on the way and then dying in great numbers when they got here.

DB *In that same Dershowitz column, he talks about the uniqueness of the Jewish Holocaust in terms of genocide, that it stands by itself. Would you accept that?*

It depends on what you mean by "unique." Every genocide obviously stands by itself in that every genocide has its own peculiar historical characteristics. But I think it is wrong to take any one genocide and concentrate on it to the neglect of others and act as if there has only been one great genocide in the world and nobody should bring up any other because it's a poor analogy. The greatest gift the Jews could give to the world is not to remember Hitler's genocide for exactly what it was, that is, the genocide of Jews, but to take what that horrible experience was for Jews and then to apply it to all the other things that are going on in the world, where huge numbers of people are dying for no reason at all. Apply it to the starvation in Somalia and the way people are treated by the advanced industrial countries in the Third World, where huge numbers of people die in wars or for economic reasons. I think in that sense what happened in the Holocaust is not unique. It should not be left alone. It should be applied everywhere it can, because that is past. The other genocides are present and future.

DB *Let's talk a little about Hollywood and history. Michael Parenti, in his book* Make Believe Media, *suggests that in an increasingly non-literate society, film has the "last frame," the last chapter of history. I'd like you to consider that in relation to Oliver Stone's docudrama* JFK. *Stone says, "The American people deserve to have their history back." What about the assumption that history was once ours and is now lost?*

Of course, it was never ours. History has always belonged to the people who controlled whatever present there was. They control history. So it's not a matter of taking it back. Very often people will say, Let us restore America to what it once was. To what? Slavery? Let us restore the good old days? The good old days lie ahead. Film is tremendously important. I don't know whether it's the last frame. I'm even dubious about whether films, as powerful as they are at the moment that they capture you, have the lasting effect that literature and writing have. I don't know this for sure. We have fewer and fewer people reading books. Are the statistics on that clear? I know everybody says this. I know that students are not reading books the way they used to. I know there are millions of people in this country who read books, and obviously many more millions who don't. In that sense it's true. They are watching videos and television and going to the movies. People who are not reached by books have only videos, movies and television. Then they become especially important. I agree with the importance of the visual media. I love the movies. I'm very happy when I see a movie made that I think does something to advance people's social consciousness. I have a special place in my heart for movies that have something important to say. When I saw Oliver Stone's movie *Salvador* I thought it was a very powerful statement about the brutal American policy supporting the dictatorship and the death squads of El Salvador. When I saw *Born on the Fourth of July*, I thought, This is great. He's bringing the antiwar movement before millions of people and showing that there's no conflict between soldiers in Vietnam and the antiwar movement. Soldiers came back from Vietnam and joined the antiwar movement, as Ron Kovic did. When I saw *JFK* I did not have the same feeling. I thought he was contradicting what he was doing in *Born on the Fourth of July*, where he was saying, We had an antiwar movement in this country. If the war came to an end, it was in good part because people like Ron Kovic and Vietnam veterans and all the other people who protested against the war showed us what a social movement was like. But in *JFK* he is telling us that the key to ending the war was the President of the United States. If Kennedy had lived he would have ended the war. That viewpoint perpetuates an elitist notion in history which I've been struggling against. I think that Oliver Stone in his better films is also struggling against it, the idea that history is made from the top, and if we want change to come about we must depend on our presidents, or the Supreme Court, or Congress. If history shows anything, to me, it shows that we cannot depend on those people on top to make the necessary changes towards justice and peace. It's social movements we must depend on to do that.

DB *What do you think about the honesty of mixing actual historical archival footage with fabricated footage?*

I think it's OK so long as the fictional pieces don't distort the history. If the fictional pieces enhance the facts, then it's fine.

DB *We've gone back and forth between some of your personal history and the politics of history. I'd like to end this interview talking about a period that had a profound impact on your life, being a bombardier in World War Two. Two missions in particular affected you deeply, one over Pilsen in Czechoslovakia and the other in France in the town of Royan. Why are they so important to you?*

These things weren't important at the time. I was another member of the Air Force doing my duty, listening to my briefings before going out on the flight and dropping the bombs where I was supposed to, without thinking, where am I dropping them? What am I doing? Who lives here? What's going on here? I flew the last missions of the war. By then we were well into Germany. We were running out of targets, and so we were bombing Eastern Europe. I remember the raid on Pilsen. A lot of planes went over. I remember reading about the raid after the war. It was described by Churchill in his memoirs as, Well, we bombed Pilsen and there were very few civilian casualties. Then I was in Europe years after that, sometime in the mid-1960s, in Yugoslavia. I ran into a couple from Pilsen. Hesitantly, I told them that I had been in one of the crews that bombed Pilsen. They said, When you finished the streets were full of corpses, hundreds and hundreds of people killed in that raid. It was only after the war that I began to think about the raids I had been on. The thing about being in the Air Force and dropping bombs from 35,000 feet is that you don't see any human beings. You don't hear screams, see blood, see mangled bodies. I understand very well how atrocities are committed in modern warfare, from a distance. So there I was doing these things.

The raid on Royan was an even more difficult experience for me as I thought about it later. It was carried out when the war was just about over. We thought we weren't going to fly any more missions, because we had already overrun France and taken most of Germany. There was virtually nothing left to bomb, and everybody knew the war was going to be over in a few weeks. We were awakened at one in the morning, the usual waking up time if you're going to fly at six. It's not like in the movies where you leap out of bed into the cockpit, rev up the engines and you're off. Five boring hours of listening to briefings, getting your equipment, putting on your electrically heated suit, going to the bombardiers' briefing, the officers' briefing, going to eat and deciding whether you eat square eggs or round eggs. They briefed us and told us we were going to bomb Royan, a little town on the Atlantic coast near Bordeaux. They showed it to us on the map. Nobody asked why. You don't ask questions at briefings. To this day I feel ashamed that it didn't even occur to me to ask, Why are we doing this when the war is almost over? Why are we bombing this little French town when France is all ours? There were a few thousand German soldiers holed up near this town, waiting for the war to end, not doing anything, not bothering anybody. But we were going to destroy them.

I didn't know at the time how many bombers were sent. All I knew was my squadron of twelve bombers was going over. I could see other squadrons. It wasn't until later, when I did research, that I learned that it was twelve hundred heavy bombers going over against two or three thousand German soldiers. But they told us in the briefing, You're going to carry a different kind of bomb. Not the usual demolition type. You're going to carry canisters, long cylinders of jellied gasoline. It didn't mean anything to us, except we knew jellied gasoline would ignite. It was napalm.

It was only after the war that I began to think about that raid and did some research and visited Royan. I went to the rebuilt library and read what they had written about it. I wrote an essay about that bombing. It epitomized the stupidity of modern warfare and how the momentum of military machines carries armies on to do the most atrocious things that any rational person sitting down for five minutes and thinking about it would stop immediately. So we destroyed the town, the German soldiers, the French also who were there. In one of my essays I coupled it with the bombing of Hiroshima as two bombings that at the time, I am ashamed to say, I welcomed. With Royan it wasn't that I welcomed it, I was just doing it. With Hiroshima I welcomed it because it meant that the war would end and I wouldn't have to go to the Pacific and fly any more bombing missions.

DB *Some years after that, in the mid-1960s, you visited Hiroshima. You had intended to make certain remarks at a gathering of survivors. You weren't able to make them.*

It was a terrible moment. A few Americans visited Hiroshima every August. It was an international gathering to commemorate the dropping of the bomb. We were taken to visit a house where people who had survived Hiroshima gathered and socialized with one another. We were a little international group, a few Americans, a Frenchman and a Russian. The Japanese survivors were sitting on the floor. We were expected to get up and say something to them as visitors from other countries. The Russian woman spoke about what the Russians had suffered in the war and how she could commiserate with the Japanese. As I planned to get up and speak, I thought, I don't know what I can say. But I have to be honest. I have to say I was a bombardier, even though I didn't bomb Japan. I bombed people, innocent people, civilians, just as in Hiroshima. So I got up to speak and looked out at the people sitting there. Suddenly something happened to my eyesight, my brain. I saw this blur of people who were blind, with missing arms, missing legs, people whose skin was covered with sores. This was real. That's what these people looked like. I looked out at them and I couldn't speak. In all the speaking I've ever done, nothing like that has ever happened to me. It was impossible. I just stood there. My voice choked up. That was it, I just couldn't speak.

How Social Change Happens

December 16, 1996

DB *I was just looking at a book of poetry of Langston Hughes. You had an opportunity to meet while you were at Spelman College in Atlanta. Do you remember that?*

Do I remember that? I'm the one who told you about that! I could have pretended to your audience that you just know all these things. But I told you that I met Langston Hughes, because I tell everybody I've met important people, whether I've met them or not. I actually did meet Langston Hughes. Not a serious meeting. It's not like when you and I sit down together and have cappuccino at the Cafe Algiers in Cambridge. This wasn't like that at all. I was teaching at Spelman. They invited him down to the Atlanta University Center. I was dispatched to pick him up at the airport, which I think I've told you is my claim to being a revolutionary. I pick people up at the airport. Sometimes even bring them back to the airport. So I picked him up at the airport and spent a little time with him, a great guy. I love his poetry. Class-conscious, simple, clear, strong. I quote it whenever I can.

DB *He was an ally of the anti-fascist forces in Spain as well. He went to Spain.*

That's right. There are pictures of him speaking in Spain. He suffered because of his left-wing connections. They put a lot of pressure on him and so he had a hard time. I think at one point in his life he relented and tried to move away from that to protect himself. He was vulnerable in many ways. His personal life made him vulnerable.

DB *Because he was gay?*

Exactly, because he was gay. It's bad enough in our time, but in that time to be gay, forget it.

DB *You've used "Ballad of the Landlord."*

"Ballad of the Landlord" is one of my favorite poems because it's so ferociously class-conscious. Maybe you'd like to read it. Do you know that this is the poem that got Jonathan Kozol fired from his job here in Boston? I guess that's what attracted me to the poem. I said, Any poem that can get anybody fired is worth paying attention to.

DB   *Jonathan Kozol, a National Book Award winner and noted educator, was fired for reading the poem?*

Yes, he got fired. College professors can be fired for what they do, but it's always done very indirectly because universities are supposed to be places of free inquiry. But elementary schools and middle schools and high schools make no pretense. They are totalitarian places, and they don't make any claim to anything else. After all, they say, these are very young minds. We mustn't expose them to class conflict. We mustn't make them think that the country is run by the rich. We mustn't give them the idea that you should oppose your landlord and fight eviction, which is what happens in this poem.

DB   *Do you want to read it?*

I'll tell you what. Let's both read it. We'll have a duet. You read one and I'll read the other.

DB   *"Ballad of the Landlord," by Langston Hughes.*

Landlord, landlord, my roof has sprung a leak.
Don't you 'member I told you about it way last week?

Landlord, landlord, these steps is broken down.
When you come up yourself it's a wonder you don't fall down.

Ten bucks you say I owe you?
Ten bucks you say is due?
That's ten bucks more'n I'll pay you
Till you fix this house up new.

What? You're gonna get eviction orders?
You're gonna to cut off my heat?
You're gonna to take my furniture
And throw it in the street?

Um-huh! You talking high and mighty.
Talk on till you get through.
You ain't gonna to be able to say a word
If I land my fist on you.

Police! Police! come and get this man!
He's trying to ruin the government
And overturn the land!

Copper's whistle! patrol bell! arrest

Precinct station.
Iron cell.
Headlines in press:

MAN THREATENS LANDLORD
TENANT HELD. NO BAIL.
JUDGE GIVES NEGRO
90 DAYS IN COUNTY JAIL.

What an incendiary poem. It's a poem about civil disobedience. Challenging a law, but so obviously you being right and them being wrong. So you don't want young kids to hear that. So if a teacher reads that to young kids, or has them read it, he's got to go. So Jonathan Kozol went. But he had his revenge. He wrote this book (*Death at an Early Age*) which brought this to the attention of an awful lot of people.

DB *His subsequent books on education,* Savage Inequalities *and* Amazing Grace, *are very powerful works.*

He's a wonderfully eloquent and passionate person about poverty and inequality and racism. That connection between him and Langston Hughes was a good one.

DB *Perhaps Langston Hughes' most famous poem is "Raisin In the Sun. A Dream Deferred." Why don't you read that?*

I think I quote that. I shouldn't say that, "I *think* I quote that." We always say that in modesty. I *know* I quote that in *A People's History of the United States* when I start talking about the movement of the 1960s and how much led up to it in black poetry and literature.

Some of the people know that title "Raisin In the Sun" because there's this famous play by Lorraine Hansberry and Sidney Poitier starred in this famous movie and on television and all that, but not a lot of people know that it came from Langston Hughes.

What happens to a dream deferred?

Does it dry up
like a raisin in the sun?
Or fester like a sore—
And then run?

Does it stink like rotten meat?
Or crust and sugar over—
like a syrupy sweet?

Maybe it just sags like a heavy load.

Or does it explode?

His language is so simple but so powerful. That image of all of that pent-up explosion. Richard Wright sort of did the same thing. Richard Wright always talked about that pent-up anger in the black population. In *Black Boy*, in which he talks about growing up in the South and what he went through and the humiliation and looking around him and seeing all the black people are toeing the line out of necessity, out of self-protection, but thinking, Something's going to happen here.

DB   *Speaking of something that's going to happen here, Hughes asks, What happens to a dream deferred? Does it explode if that dream is not realized? In late October in Boulder you said that, "We can't go on with the present polarization of wealth and poverty."*

I don't know how long we can go on, but I know we can't go on indefinitely. That growing gap between wealth and poverty is a recipe for trouble, for disaster, for conflict, for explosion. Here's the Dow

Jones average going up, up, up and there are the lives of people in the city. The Dow Jones average in the last fifteen years has gone up 400%. In the same period, the wages of working people, of 80% of the population, have gone down 15%. 400% up, 15% down. Now the richest 1% of the population owning 43%, 44% of the wealth. Up from the usual maybe 28%, 30%, 32%, which is bad enough and which has been a constant throughout American history. In fact it's been so constant that when they did studies of the tax rolls in Boston in the seventeenth and eighteenth centuries, they concluded that 1% of the population owned 33% of the wealth. If you look at the statistics all through American history, you see that figure, a little more, a little less, around the same. Now it's even worse and worse. So something's got to give.

DB *Given that enormous growth in income and wealth, the inequality, if you were a member, let's say, of the ruling class, I know you're not, that's why I say if—*

How do you know I'm not?

DB *You're just a historian, retired, professor emeritus. But let's say if you were, wouldn't this trend toward increasing polarization give you cause for concern? Because for you to keep your power and privilege you need stability. You don't need unrest and upheaval.*

That's true. But there's always this conflict within the ruling class. The people who know this from a long-term point of view say, Hey, we'd better do something about it. That's why you see people up there in the ruling class, that's your phrase, "ruling class." I would never use a class-conscious phrase like that. But you used it, so I can use it. The ruling class. There have always been some members of the ruling class who wanted reforms, who wanted to ease things, who worried about a future explosion. These are the people who supported Roosevelt. They were members of the ruling class who supported Roosevelt and the New Deal reforms because they knew that they couldn't let things go on the way they were, with the turmoil of the 1930s, that there was a revolution brewing. So there have always been people like that. I think of Felix Rohatyn, who's this big banker. He says, Let's not go on like this. This polarization of wealth is going too far. But on the other hand, there are all those other greedy ones. They want it now. They think of the short term. OK, maybe there'll be rebellion against my grandchildren. It shows how their family values operate. They don't care if the rebellion takes place against their grandchildren. But now I'm going to haul in as much as I can. And that's what they're doing.

DB   *I'm saving the easy questions as we proceed into the interview. How does social change happen?*

Thanks. I can deal with that in thirty seconds. You think I know? We know how it has happened, and we can sort of extrapolate from that, not that you can extrapolate mathematically, but you can sort of get suggestions from that. You see change happening when there has been an accumulation of grievance until it reaches a boiling point. Then something happens. When I say, look at historical situations and try to extrapolate from that, what happens in the South in the 1950s and 1960s? It's not that suddenly black people were put back into slavery. It's not as if there was some precipitating thing that suddenly pushed them back. They were, as the Southern white ruling class was eager to say, making progress. It was glacial progress, extremely slow. But they were making progress. But it's not the absolute amount of progress that's made that counts. It's the amount of progress made against what the ideal should be in the minds of the people who are aggrieved. And the ideal in the minds of the black people was, We have to be equal. We have to be treated as equals. The progress that was being made in the South was so far from that. The recognition of that gap between what should be and what is, which existed for a long time but waited for a moment when a spark would be lit. The thing about sparks being lit is that you never know what spark is going to ignite and really result in a conflagration. After all, before the Montgomery bus boycott there had been other boycotts. Before the sit-ins of the 1960s, there had been between 1955 and 1960 sit-ins in sixteen different cities which nobody paid any attention to and which did not ignite a movement. But then in Greensboro, on February 1, 1960, these four college kids go in, sit in, and everything goes haywire. Then things are never the same. You never know, and this is I think an encouragement to people who do things, not knowing whether they will result in anything, and you do things again and again and nothing happens, that you have to do things, do things, do things, you have to light that match, light that match, light that match, not knowing how often it's going to sputter and go out and at what point it's going to take hold, at what point other people, seeing what happens, are going to be encouraged, provoked to do the same. That's what happened in the civil rights movement and that's what happens in other movements. Things take a long time. It requires patience, but not a passive patience, the patience of activism.

When I was in South Africa in 1982, I was invited there to give a lecture to the University of Capetown. At the time, apartheid defined the country, Mandela was in Robben's Island, the African National Congress was outlawed, people were being banned. We know about books being banned, there, it was people who were banned. They couldn't speak. They couldn't go here or there. The secret police everywhere. Just before I arrived at the University of Capetown the secret police of South Africa had just broken into the offices of the student newspaper at the University and made off with all of their stuff. It was the kind of thing that happened all the time. The atmosphere was an atmosphere of terror. You would think perhaps, only seeing that, nothing is going to happen here, like you would think in the South in the early 1950s. You don't see any sign of a civil rights revolution in the South in the early 1950s. But having come from that experience in the South, I became aware, just talking to people, going to meetings, going to a huge rally outside of Johannesburg, where everybody did everything illegal, where they sang the anthem of the African National Congress, raised the flags of the African National Congress, where banned people spoke. I suddenly was aware that underneath the surface of total control things were simmering, things were going on. I didn't know when it would break through, but we saw it break through not long ago. Suddenly Mandela comes out of Robben's Island and becomes President of the new South Africa. We should be encouraged. We shouldn't be discouraged. We should be encouraged by historical examples of social change, by how surprising changes take place suddenly, when you least expect it, not because of a miracle from on high, but because people have labored patiently for a long time.

DB *Do you think it's important to rethink the way we think about time? Everyone's in a hurry. Well, this change you're suggesting, Professor, I'm a very busy guy. I've got about fifteen minutes.*

It's true. We have to rethink the whole question of time. We have to get used to the idea that the great society—I'm sorry to use that phrase. All those phrases were OK: the Great Society, the New Frontier, the New Deal. They weren't realized. We have to get accustomed to the idea that it may not come in our lifetime. We will see changes in our lifetime. Who knows what we will see? Think of Mandela, in prison for decades. Think of people in the South living in humiliation for a hundred years, waiting. I'm not saying it will take a hundred years or it will take decades. I don't know how long it will take for important changes to take place. You never know. But when people get discouraged because they do something and nothing happens, they should really understand that the only way things will happen is if people get over the notion that they must see immediate success. If they get over that notion and persist, then they will see things happen before they even realize it.

DB   *Was your job at Spelman College in Atlanta the first job you got when you got out of the university?*

I call it my first "real" teaching job. I had a number of unreal teaching jobs. By unreal I mean I was teaching part-time at Upsala College in New Jersey.

DB   *Now bankrupt, incidentally.*

Because I taught there?

DB   *This just happened. Literally, colleges are now going bankrupt.*

I said patience. It took a while after I was there to reap the fruits of my being there and go bankrupt. I wouldn't be surprised if every other place that I've touched goes bankrupt. I have written articles for a number of magazines. Those magazines are now defunct. I'm warning you about what will happen to Alternative Radio after this interview. You never know.

DB   *I'll take my chances.*

I taught at Upsala College. How do you know about all these defunct places? Do you have a list? Anyway, I did teach there part-time. Maybe it's defunct because it was very Lutheran. So strict. It was like being back in the time of Luther, back in the sixteenth century. But in any case, I had a part-time job there and a part-time job at Brooklyn College. But Spelman College was my first full-time teaching job. I immediately catapulted from graduate student at Columbia University to chair—I want you to take full cognizance of that—of a department. Four persons in the department. Like being head waiter in a two-waiter restaurant. Not just history. Four persons included everything: history, political science, sociology, philosophy. Four people doing all of that. We were renaissance people.

DB *What year was that?*

That was in 1956 when my wife Roz and my two kids Myla and Jeff—mind if I mention their names? I want to give them air time—all trundled into our old Chevy, went down.

DB *I assume it was in terms of your socialization a rather radicalizing experience for you. I presume you lived in a black neighborhood near the college.*

Actually, the first year we were there—we were there a total of seven—we lived in a white, working-class neighborhood on the edge of Atlanta, which was an interesting experience in itself. We weren't far from Stone Mountain, which is a Ku Klux Klan gathering place. We were living in this first house we'd ever lived in. We had always lived in the slums in New York or in low-income housing projects. Here we were in a little house like the other little houses on this block of working-class white people. One of the first things that happened when we were there is we hear all this noise. We go outside. There was a main street about a block from our house. There was a parade of people with white hoods, KKK, marching to Stone Mountain.

We spent a year there. It was sort of inconvenient traveling back and forth. We moved to the Spelman College campus, which was surrounded by a black community. We lived essentially in the black community for the next six years. You say radicalizing experience? I guess so. Of course I like to think that I was a radical even before I came to Spelman College. But we all like to pretend that we were radical at the age of three, right? You might say I had been radicalized by working in the shipyards, but maybe a little more radicalized by being in a war. But probably that time at Spelman College was the most intense experience of learning in my life. I think it's fair to say that. Talk about social change, I could see social change happening all around me and then writing about it, observing it, participating in it, seeing my Spelman College students so controlled in that old guard atmosphere of the old South in which students, especially young black women, were being trained to take their obedient places in the segregated society. Trained to pour tea and wear white gloves and march into and out of chapel and really to be kept inside this kind of nunnery. Then suddenly to see them break out of this when they look at television and watch the sit-ins taking place in Greensboro and Rock Hill, South Carolina and Nashville and to see them gathering. Julian Bond across the street at Morehouse College meeting with Lonnie King, the football captain at Morehouse College, gathering people from Spelman and getting together and planning the first sit-ins in the spring of 1960 in Atlanta. My students literally leaping over that stone wall that surrounded the Spelman campus and doing what they weren't supposed to do. Seeing this remarkable change in them, this growth of courage and getting arrested, going to jail. Marian Wright Edelman, my student at Spelman, going to jail. A photo of her appearing in the newspapers the next day showing this very studious Spelman student behind bars reading a book which she had brought along with her so she wouldn't miss her class or homework. Seeing the South change in that time, seeing white Southerners change, seeing white Southerners get used to the idea that the South is going to change and accepting it.

DB *What I meant by radicalizing you, I was thinking in terms of being a witness to an oppressive mechanism, segregation, U.S.-style apartheid, Jim Crow, and then watching the resistance to it grow.*

Anybody who was in any way in the U.S. socially conscious knew vaguely that there was racial segregation. But to be right there and to witness it in action, to talk to my students about their early lives, about the first time they realized that they were black and being considered different and treated differently. To participate in sit-ins and to see the atmosphere around us in Rich's Department Store suddenly change from friendly to hostile when four of us, two black and two white, my wife and I and two black students from Spelman, sit down in this lunch counter at Rich's. Suddenly it's as if a bomb had been dropped or plague had been visited on it. The people gathering around us and shouting and cursing. Getting an inkling, being white people, just an inkling, of what it is to be black and be subject all your life to the thought that if you step one foot out of line you'll be surrounded by people who are threatening you. That's a learning experience. Learning comes in layers. There's something you think you know? You don't know it until you see it very up close, penetrating you. So it was a learning experience.

I learned a lot about teaching, too. I learned that the most important thing about teaching is not what you do in the classroom but what you do outside of the classroom and what you do to bring the lessons of books and the writings of thinkers and the facts of history, what you do to make a connection between that and the world outside. To go outside the classroom yourself, to bring your students outside the classroom, or to have them bring you outside the classroom, because very often they do it first and you say, I can't hang back. I'm their teacher. I have to be there with them. And to learn that the best kind of teaching is the one that makes this connection between social action and book learning.

DB *Why do you think so many of your colleagues, and I think this is a fair statement to make, really want to just busy themselves with their scholarship and turning out papers and attending conferences? I'm not saying that doesn't have any value. But when it comes to "out there," to being engaged with what's happening in the streets, in society, they don't feel it's appropriate.*

There's a powerful drive in our society for safety and security. And everybody is vulnerable because we all are part of a hierarchy of power in which unless we're at the very, very top, unless we're billionaires, or the President of the U.S., or the boss, and very few of us are bosses, we are somewhere on some lower rung in the hierarchy of power, where somebody has power over us, somebody has the power to fire us, to withhold a raise, to punish us in some way. Here in this rich country, so prideful of the economic system, the most prominent, the most clear-cut thing you can say about this great economic success is that everybody is insecure. Everybody is nervous. Even if you're doing well, you're nervous. Something will happen to you. In fact, the people who are doing fairly well, the middle class, are more nervous than the people at the bottom, who know what to expect and have smaller expectations. There's this nervousness, this insecurity, and this economic fear of saying the wrong thing, doing the wrong thing, stepping out of line. The academic world has its own special culture of conformity and being professional. All the professions have the cult of professionalism, even in your profession, radio broadcasters. Being professional means not being committed.

DB   *Not having an agenda.*

Right. There are people who might call you unprofessional, because sometimes I suspect you have an agenda. Sometimes I suspect you care about what's going on in the world. Sometimes I suspect that the people you interview are the people whose ideas you want to broadcast. You're not supposed to do that. It's unprofessional. It's unprofessional to be a teacher who goes out on picket lines, or who even invites students out on picket lines. It's unprofessional to be a teacher who says to students, Look, instead of giving you a final exam, your assignment for the semester is to go out into the community and work with some organization that you believe in and then do a report on that instead of taking a final exam of multiple choice questions asking you who was President during the Mexican War. So that's unprofessional. And you will stand out. You will stick out if the stuff you write is not written for scholarly journals but is written for everybody to read, because certainly the stuff written for scholarly journals is not written for everybody to read. It's deliberately written in such a way that not everybody can read it. Very few people can read it. So if you write stuff that the ordinary person can read, you're suspect. They'll say you're not a scholar, you're a journalist. Or you're not a scholar, you're a propagandist, because you have a point of view. They don't have a point of view. Scholarly articles don't have a point of view. Of course, they really do. They have an agenda. But they don't say it. They may not even know they have an agenda. The agenda is obedience. The agenda is silence. The agenda is safety. The agenda is, Don't rock the boat.

DB   *One of the criticisms of* Alternative Radio *that I hear from program directors around the country is that it's "not objective." It's not balanced. These are terms of abuse in order to actually limit the possibility of people actually hearing dissenting voices such as yours.*

This business of "balance" is very funny. What is balance? The *MacNeil/Lehrer NewsHour* is balanced, right? They have people on the far right balanced by people on the not-so-far right balanced by people in the middle balanced by one person two degrees to the left of the middle. That's balanced. If you said to MacNeil/Lehrer, Why don't you have Noam Chomsky on as a regular commentator to balance all the Assistant Secretaries of State and the Secretaries of Defense and the Congressmen, just one person to balance hundreds of others? They would say, No, that's not what we mean by balance.

The fact is, things are already unbalanced. The pretense is that things are balanced and you want to keep them that way. But of course they're already so far out of balance, we would have to put an enormous amount of left-wing weight onto the scales in order even to make the scales move slightly towards balance.

DB *You just mentioned that MIT professor Noam Chomsky. When did you first meet Chomsky?*

I first met Noam—do you mind if I call him Noam? I call you David.

DB *Very familiar.*

Very familiar. Unprofessional. I first met Noam, I had moved not long before to Boston from the South. It was the summer of 1965. I had vaguely heard of him from somebody who talked about him as a linguist. I knew there was a guy named Chomsky at MIT and that he was brilliant in the field of linguistics. That's all I knew about him. I didn't know that he had any interest in politics. This is a funny thing to say. If somebody said today about Noam Chomsky, Oh, I didn't know that he was interested in politics, well! And then, something was happening. I moved out of the South but I was still in touch with things in the region. A lot of people were being arrested in Jackson, Mississippi, black people, SNCC people, and being held in the big compound because there were too many of them to fit into the jails. It was decided to send a delegation of people from the Boston area down to take a look at things and make a report. Bob Zellner, one of the original SNCC people, one of the few white people in SNCC, a white Southerner from Alabama, a fantastic person, organized this and asked me to come. I said OK. I found myself on a plane going south sitting next to a guy who introduced himself as Noam Chomsky. A very immodest statement, don't you think, for him to say, I'm Noam Chomsky? So we talked all the way down. Then we talked while we were there and we talked on the way back. We became friends. I became aware of the fact that he was a guy who wasn't just interested in linguistics—although he had a slight interest in linguistics—but he was very, very deeply concerned about what was going on in the country and the world and it occurred to me, talking to him, that he was very smart. So from then on, and then of course with the Vietnam War escalating just about that time, the two of us found ourselves on the same platform again and again at the same rallies. So we got to know one another.

DB *You've said that you were often the opening act for Chomsky.*

Like rock and roll groups. I was the warm-up. I had a lot of emotional statements surrounding several facts. Noam would come on with one vaguely emotional statement and 7,000 facts. It seemed to me a good combination.

DB *As you know, he's not a flamboyant, charismatic speaker. He would be the first to acknowledge that. What accounts for the enormous crowds that he attracts, not just in the U.S. but all around the world?*

You say, Not just in the U.S. He attracts bigger crowds in Canada and in Europe and now lately in Latin America. I just talked to him today. He just returned from Latin America. Everywhere he goes there are huge crowds. Everywhere I go to speak, five hundred people show up. They inform me quietly, Noam Chomsky was here two weeks ago. Two thousand people came to hear him. Is this a message they're trying to give me? I'm inadequate? The reason so many people turn out to hear him is one, they've heard about him. I guess he's famous. It's interesting that he should be famous, because all the organs of power in the U.S. are trying their best not to make him famous, to shut him up, not to publish him, not to pay attention to him, not to put him on national radio or TV. But his message has been so powerful and so outrageously true and so backed up by information and so very often ahead of everybody else. Look, he was the first one in this country to talk about East Timor. Now the East Timor rebels get the Nobel Prize. As I go around the country, wherever I go

Noam has already spoken or is about to speak there. Plus he speaks at a lot of places where I don't speak. I have run into so many people all over who say that they went to hear him speak and it had an amazing effect on them, as you say, without him being flamboyant. Just the power of what he says, the information that piles up, so devastating and so obviously true, and with such documentation. It amounts to a powerful indictment of our society, of our economic system, of our political system, of the hypocrisy, of the failure of the press to report what is going on in the world. To me it's a very encouraging thing that wherever Noam speaks huge crowds turn out. It shows me that there is an enormous population in this country that is hungry for information that they don't get in the major media.

Another encouraging thing to me is the alternate radio and alternate media. I can't tell you how many people have said to me, I know you think I'm buttering you up, yes, I guess I am buttering you up. Call it margarine, it's the New Age. People say to me, Hey, I heard the talk you gave. And they mention some radio station somewhere that I never heard of and apparently you have this satellite that's floating around. You bounce a talk by Noam Chomsky or by me or by Barbara Ehrenreich off these satellites and they go out to radio stations. You notice how technologically astute I am in my accurate description of exactly how this thing works? It bounces off the satellite, goes to these radio stations and then into people's homes? Isn't that how it works exactly?

DB *So despite what the pundits are telling us about the population being passive and quiescent, you think there's an audience there for dissidence?*

Absolutely. I talk very often to captive audiences. Not prisoners, I mean people who turn out to hear me talk, and I imagine this is even more true of the larger crowds that turn out to hear Noam. These are not the radicals of the community. Five hundred people come to hear me in Duluth, Minnesota. There are not five hundred radicals in Duluth, Minnesota who have come to hear me tell them what they already know. I don't know why they're there. Maybe there's not a lot to do in Duluth that night. That seems like an insult to Duluth. There are a few things to do. Who knows why? What I'm trying to say is they're not people who are already aficionados of the left and of radical messages. They come maybe out of curiosity. Their interest has been piqued by an article in the newspaper or whatever and they come to hear me. Then I deliver what I believe is a radical message: this is what's wrong with our economic system. It's fundamental. This is what's wrong with our political system. It's fundamental. We need to redistribute the wealth in this country. We need to use it in a rational way. We need to take this enormous arms budget and not just cut it slightly but dismantle it because we have to make up our minds we're not going to go to war any more. We're not going to militarily intervene anymore. If we're not going to go to war any more, then we have $250 billion. Then we don't have to worry about Medicare, Social Security, child care, universal health care, education. We can have a better society. I say things which if you mentioned them to MacNeil/Lehrer they would say, That's a little too much for our listeners. It's not too much. I think this is what Noam does too. You tell people what makes common sense, it makes common sense that if you're a very, very rich country nobody in the country should be hungry. Nobody should be homeless. Nobody should be without health care. The richest country in the world. Nobody should be without these things. We have the resources but they're being wasted or given somewhere to somebody. It's common sense. So there are people all over this country, millions of people, who would listen to such a message and say, yes, yes, yes. The problem is to organize these people into a movement.

DB *Mike Moore, the celebrated film director of* Roger and Me *and of* TV Nation *very effectively uses humor to convey political ideas, as does Molly Ivins and Jim Hightower and yourself. Do you feel that humor is a way to maybe hook a larger audience and to make left, progressive ideas more attractive?*

I don't like to think of it that way. I don't go home and say, I think we've got to reach people, so I'll try to get humorous. Rather, it's a way of having a little fun with the world in a world that is not giving us a lot of fun, that's giving us tragedy, pictures of hungry people and pictures of war. Maybe it's something I learned from being in the South and being in the black community, to see how much humor there was among people who you might say have no right to laugh. There's nothing to laugh about, and these people are laughing and having fun. Or people in the army, people at war. They've got to have humor. They've got to have fun. They need to laugh. We've got to have fun even while we're dealing with serious things. We've got to represent in the present what we want in the future. I suppose that's why we do that. It's not a planned conspiracy.

DB *Have you noticed any changes in your profession, history? I hesitate to use the term "revisionist," because it smacks of the Soviet era. But along the lines of* A People's History, *your book, there's James Loewen's book* Lies My Teacher Told Me. *Have there been some changes in this area?*

No question there have been changes. Obviously not enough to say, The teaching of history has changed. But obviously enough changes to alarm the right wing in this country, to alarm the American Legion, to alarm senators, to alarm Lynne Cheney, Robert Dole, William Bennett, Gertrude Himmelfarb, and to alarm all these people who are holding on to the old history. They're alarmed because there have been changes. The story of Columbus has changed now, not in the majority of schools around the country, but in thousands. This is alarming. What? Young kids are going to begin to think of Columbus as not just an adventurer, but as a predator, a kidnapper, an enslaver, a torturer, a bad person and think maybe that conquest and expansion are not good things and that the search for gold is not something to be welcomed? Kids, be happy! Gold has been found! No, greed is no good. And maybe, let's take a look at the Indian societies that Columbus came upon. How did they live? How did they treat one another? Columbus stories that are told in the schools don't usually include stories of how the Indians were living on this continent.

Somebody sent me a letter reminding me of the work of William Brandon. He has done research for decades about Indians and their communities on this hemisphere before Columbus came and after. His research was in the French archives because he works in France. The reports came back from the French missionaries, the Jesuits, on how the Indians live. It's an amazing story and one that would make anybody question capitalism, greed, competition, disparate wealth, hierarchy. To start to hint about that, telling a new kind of Columbus story, a new kind of Native American story, is subversive of the way things are. Also, the Reconstruction period is being told in a new way. Eric

Foner's book *Reconstruction* is marvelous. It's a very different treatment of Reconstruction and the books on Reconstruction that existed when I was going to graduate school in the 1950s, where incidentally they did not put on my reading list W.E.B. Du Bois' *Black Reconstruction*, which you might say is an earlier version of Eric Foner's book, at least a vital predecessor to it. So a lot of history teaching has changed. Not enough yet. We need to do a lot more. But just enough to frighten the keepers of the old.

DB *We had an opportunity in late October to visit the new maximum security prison in Florence, Colorado. It was a rather extraordinary trip.*

Don't deny the fact that you drove the getaway car. Also the get-there car. I didn't have a car at my disposal, I was speaking in Boulder, and I had this old friend of mine in prison, in this maximum maximum, they call it "ad max" security federal prison in southern Colorado. It was good that we had a lot of fun on the way, because when we got there it was no fun. Grim. Frightening. Something out of some fantasy of totalitarianism. New. Technologically admirable. But holding these prisoners in such a tight grip. The man that I visited I've known for twenty-five years, and he is actually an extraordinary human being. There are some extraordinary human beings behind bars. Sure, there are mad killers and rapists. There are those. But there are also extraordinary people behind bars who shouldn't be there. He is one of them. I could not shake hands with him when I visited. We were separated by this glass wall. We had to talk through these phones. So there's no contact. It's called a no-contact visit. Yet, although there is no contact, there's all this between us, before he comes out to see me he is strip-searched by the guards. After he sees me he is strip-searched again by the guards. That's humiliating, taking all his clothes off, inspecting all the cavities of his body. Assuming that I, Houdini-like, have managed to slip things through the glass to him which will enable him to escape from there. It was a nightmare. What was amazing was that not everybody commits suicide in a situation like that, that somebody like my friend Jimmy Barrett, and I think it's because of his social consciousness, has the strength to withstand that. You talk about patience. Jimmy says: Patience. Things will change. I will get out of here and things will be different.

DB   *I was wondering also about the larger societal message that a building like that sends. I was sitting in the lobby while you were inside talking to your friend. What do I see? An incredible building costing a lot of money, with tiled inlaid floors, high ceilings, huge glass windows, smiling photos of Clinton and Janet Reno and the prison warden and assistant warden. You see in the back "Florence ADX. First in Security." While I was sitting there waiting for you I had a very mischievous thought that I'd like to connect the words "in" and "security" together. What struck me was that about the same time that we were there the* New York Times, *a well-known source of radical information, reported that kids in the New York City public school system, the largest one in the country, were meeting in gymnasiums, cafeterias, and locker rooms because of overcrowding. That contrast was startling.*

I remember you pointing that out to me on our way back, which was not as fun-filled as our way there. Those ironies, those contrasts, are such as to make one think very, very hard about our society. To think that there are more young black people in prison than in college, or to think that the state of California spends more money on prisons than on schools. Or to think that it costs more to house one person in a prison than to send one person to Harvard, room and board, tuition and everything. Maybe we should have a prisoner exchange, Harvard students and prisoners, just for a little while, and see what happens.

You Can't Be Neutral on a Moving Train

February 3 and 5, 1997

DB *I want to first of all track down something that I think seems to be somewhat improbable. That is, I heard that you actually studied with the great historian from 450 BC, Herodotus.*

Herodotus studied with me. Just a small correction.

DB *One of the things that is characteristic about your work is your connection with art and poetry and films. Not a lot of historians or academics integrate culture into their work. Why do you do that?*

I think that art and politics enhance one another. Art is inevitably political—I know that's a big discussion—because it has an effect on the world and it comes out of the world as it is. I think for anybody who's interested in political and social issues, art plays a very special role in enhancing statements that otherwise would be prosaic and dull, in lending passion to something, to facts that need something more than simple statements. Movements have always been given enormous stimulus and inspiration by art and artists. The trade union movement has been helped enormously by music, by labor union songs. The civil rights movement, there's no way of escaping the power, sitting in a church in Selma, of a Selma freedom chorus in building up the courage of black people in Dallas County, knowing that the next day they were going to face state troopers and the sheriff, and the power of song just swept people into a kind of recognition that they could do what they thought they couldn't do.

DB *You were first alerted to the Ludlow Massacre in Colorado by a song by Woody Guthrie.*

That's right. Interestingly enough, I had studied history, undergraduate, graduate school, Ph.D. at Columbia, and nowhere in any of my history books, in none of my classes, did anyone ever mention the

Colorado coal strike of 1913-1914, or the Ludlow Massacre, an important point in that strike. Then I heard a song by Woody Guthrie called "The Ludlow Massacre," very haunting and powerful. It led me to begin to look into it and read about it outside of the classroom. It led me to the New York Public Library and five huge volumes of Congressional testimony about this amazing incident that took place in southern Colorado in 1913-1914.

DB   *You wrote a poem in your teens about your Uncle Phil. It's in your autobiography,* You Can't Be Neutral on a Moving Train, *in the chapter entitled "Growing Up Class-Conscious."*

It's very nice of you, David, to talk about me as writing poetry. That was a real act of arrogance to include a poem of mine in my memoir, the only poem I ever wrote. But we'll pretend it's part of an enormous number of unpublished poems which some day the world will find. I started that chapter with it because I thought that the poem—whether it really is poetry or not—says something very concisely about the circumstances in which I grew up.

DB   *Why don't you read it?*

You know this is my first poetry reading? I've always envied those people who did poetry readings; I always wished I had a poem to read. Then when I wrote this, I never thought anybody would ask me to read a poem, but I will.

Go see your Uncle Phil
And say hello.
Who would walk a mile today
To say hello,
The city freezing in the snow?

Phil had a news stand
Under the black El.
He sat on a wooden box
In the cold and in the heat.
And three small rooms across the street.

Today the wooden box was gone,
On top the stand Uncle Phil was curled.
A skeleton inside an Army coat.
He smiled and gave me a stick of gum
With stiffened fingers, red and numb.

Go see your Uncle Phil today
My mother said again in June
I walked the mile to say hello
With the city smelling almost sweet
Brand new sneakers on my feet.

The stand was nailed and boarded tight
And quiet in the sun.
Uncle Phil lay cold, asleep,
Under the black El, in a wooden box
In three small rooms across the street.

My Uncle Phil was a World War I veteran, and that's why he was able to get a newsstand. It was affirmative action. Veterans got certain things. As a veteran, he could have the right to run a newsstand, on which he made his pennies and dollars. When our family was in dire straits, Uncle Phil, as little as he had, would always come through with a little bit of cash, a little bit of help, just when we were desperate. So he held a special place in my heart.

DB *It's interesting as well, Noam Chomsky had an uncle who ran a newsstand in New York who had a big influence on him in terms of his political development.*

It wasn't Uncle Phil, was it?

DB *Let's talk a bit more about the intersection of art and politics. The era of the blacklist and the naming names of alleged communists is again in the news. Elia Kazan, a major figure in American culture in the post-World War II era, was just denied a lifetime achievement award from the American Film Institute because he named names.*

Kazan was a very, very talented director. I think it should be possible to separate out, for certain purposes and certain reasons, what people do in their art and what people do in their politics. On certain levels they can be separated. On other levels they cannot be separated. So if Elia Kazan directs a fine movie, I don't think we should refuse to see it because Elia Kazan was an informer before the House Un-American Activities Committee (HUAC). But if he's going to get some recognition, some special kind of recognition and honor, and that implies something more than a specific work of art that he is connected with, then it seems to me his whole being, his whole life becomes relevant. I would not give a medal to Leni Riefenstahl for producing even the most technically magnificent films for the Nazis. And while I wouldn't put Elia Kazan in jail for being an informer, and I wouldn't even put him on a blacklist for being an informer, even though his informing led to other people being on blacklists, special little luxuries like awards and medals are another matter. I think to deny those is a way of making a statement about informing. Every one of these awards is a statement. To give him an award in spite of what he did is to say, his giving names to HUAC wasn't very important. But to deny him an award and make the news is to say to people, No, it is a very serious thing that he did, and should be taken note of.

DB *Lillian Hellman, the playwright, called that period "scoundrel time." It wasn't quite black and white, all the good guys on one side, the people who didn't cooperate, and all the bad guys on the other side.*

That's true. There were different kinds of people who cooperated, and cooperated to different degrees. I think cooperation to the point of giving the names of other people and therefore making them subject to punishment in order to save yourself, I think that was a particularly outrageous thing to do. On the other hand, you could feel compassion for people, not admiration, only compassion, who didn't have the courage to stand up to the Committee. I remember that scene of Larry Parks, who became famous for playing Al Jolson—come to think of it, on his knees—getting on his knees, in effect, before HUAC and pleading with them not to force him, not to insist that he give names. Ultimately he did. He knew he was doing something terrible. It might warrant compassion, but it's not admirable.

DB *There's the case of Lee J. Cobb, a well-known actor. He played the benighted Willy Loman in Arthur Miller's Death of a Salesman. He also was the union mobster in Elia Kazan's On the Waterfront. He had quite an interesting experience in that gray area.*

He did inform when he spoke to the Committee. In talking to Victor Navasky for his book *Naming Names*, a remarkable book, he knew that he had done something really evil, and he acknowledged it and pointed to the fact that his being so frail still doesn't justify what he did. I had different feelings about the film *On the Waterfront* than other people on the left did. True, Kazan made a film which justified informing because Marlon Brando was a longshoreman who informed on the corrupt union officials and the corrupt bosses. The tie between the corrupt union officials and the big boys, was seen, unfortunately, only briefly in the film, just a quick shot of the rich fat cats behind the labor bosses. The labor bosses are the central evil in the film. It would have been better if it had been more of a clear partnership between the two. But I liked that film because I don't think you can take an absolute stand on any issue in which you have a reply which covers every instance. Like, under no conditions should anybody inform on anybody for any reason. We wanted people to inform on Nazis. We want people to inform on racists, on who murdered those three civil rights workers in Mississippi. So obviously each situation has to be considered differently. Marlon Brando represents the working man who faces a labor mob that kills his brother and that exploits the workers. He informs on them. That didn't strike me as a terrible thing, unless you want to make a blanket condemnation of all informing for all time. The only thing about it that I would take exception to is that he's informing on them to a government committee, which of course should not be trusted with any bit of information and cannot be counted on to do the right thing.

DB *Another work that appeared, a Broadway play, right about the time of* On the Waterfront, *was Arthur Miller's* The Crucible. *It has now been made into a film. It depicts the hysteria that engulfed Salem, Massachusetts in the seventeenth century.*

I saw *The Crucible* on stage, on Broadway. I also saw the French film version of it, which has been lost to history, and then read it. I always admired what Arthur Miller did. I have no doubt that he wrote

The Crucible out of his own experience and out of the experience of the nation. Arthur Miller was called before the House Un-American Activities Committee. He was an honorable person in refusing to do what other people had done, what Kazan had done, what Cobb had done, those people with whom he had been associated in the production of *Death of a Salesman*. I have no doubt that *The Crucible* is meant to say something not just about the witches of the seventeenth century, but about any kind of hysterical hunt for scapegoats in our time. Communists in the 1950s, and then by extension to welfare mothers today, to illegal immigrants, to anybody who becomes the object of hatred. So I think that was a wonderful work of art that Miller produced for us.

DB   *The character of Willy Loman in* Death *of a Salesman seems to be a kind of metaphor for the political economy, capitalism.*

What's interesting is that the interpretation of *Death of a Salesman* varied from person to person. There were people who did not get the anti-capitalist message from it. I remember Arthur Miller once saying that he got a huge amount of correspondence from people who had seen or read the play. He got one letter from a man who said, I agree totally with the point that you are trying to make in this play: New England is a bad territory for salesmen. But I think that letter was an exception. I think the larger message of *Death of a Salesman* is still tremendously important. Namely, a society where profit decides what happens to human beings is the essence of capitalism. Capitalism is a system that's driven by the motive of corporate profit and business profit. Profit comes first. Human beings come next. That's what happened in *Death of a Salesman*. He did it so powerfully.

DB   *And it's the real-life experience today of literally millions of Americans who have worked in some cases decades at particular offices or banks or factories and they're just discarded. Thanks, good night, Charlie.*

Willy Loman was "downsized," in contemporary terminology. That's why *Death of a Salesman* has had such universal and lasting impact, because it represents the insecurity of people under the capitalist system, the constant insecurity which attaches not just to working people and not just to the "underclass," as we call them, the people who are on the margins, but the middle class. We've seen how much economic insecurity there is today for people who are professionals, who have presumably well-paying jobs, and yet their jobs can end in a moment if their corporation decides to merge with another corporation, or to go overseas, or decides it simply doesn't need them any more.

DB *Growing up in New York in the 1930s, were you aware of what was going on in Europe, particularly in Spain with the Spanish Civil War? Were you following those things at that time?*

I was just beginning to. In 1936, when the Spanish Civil War started, I was fourteen years old. You might say the Spanish Civil War spanned my years of fourteen to seventeen. It was just the time when I was beginning to become politically aware, beginning to read books on politics, on fascism in Europe. The way the Spanish Civil War came to me was that we were playing street football. There was no such thing as a football field. We were playing tackle on the asphalt. No gear. But kids are crazy that way, or desperate. There was a guy, Jerry Weinberg, who played with us all the time, very short, very fast. Suddenly he was no longer there, he wasn't playing with us. Weeks passed. I asked, Where is Jerry Weinberg? They said, He's gone off to fight in Spain. It impressed me that he would give up our street football to fight in Spain. I read and heard more about all these young Americans who were willing to risk their lives for a cause that was taking place 3,000 miles away, that they so deeply believed in.

DB *The conventional history of the Spanish Civil War is, Had the West stood up to Franco and his allies Hitler and Mussolini, World War II would never have happened. What do you think of that?*

I don't know. I'm not sure. Could Hitler have been deterred at some early point from going into Czechoslovakia, into Austria? Perhaps. But when you go back and try to rewrite history, you're faced not with one alternative, but an endless number of permutations and combinations. There's no way really of saying what might have happened under those circumstances. But I certainly think it's fair to note that Hitler was aided in his surge towards power by the West, and of course aided at another point later by the Soviet Union. So that everybody, you might say, collaborated. All the presumably antifascist powers collaborated in allowing Hitler to rise to power.

DB *There's been some new evidence that has come out around Munich. Again, the conventional wisdom about Munich is that Chamberlain followed a policy of appeasement and had he held firm, Hitler would have been deterred. But in fact this new history that's being uncovered now suggests that it wasn't a policy of appeasement at all. It was a policy of collaboration between Britain and Nazi Germany.*

I have no doubt about that. The anticommunist feeling was so strong in the power circles of the United States, England and France that they were more concerned with the Soviet Union than they were with Nazi Germany. So in that sense, as you say, it was not simply appeasement but a collaboration. It was the balance of power tactic, which—amazingly, in a world which is so different, a world which has seen so many tragedies occur after balance of power strategies have played out—is still operative in the higher circles of political scientists and foreign policy strategists. The same balance of power concept operates when the U.S. in recent years supports Iraq against Iran and then goes to war against Iraq, and when it gives arms to Arab countries in the Middle East and gives arms to Israel, playing one against the other. What happens in the balance of power game is very often things get suddenly unbalanced, and disaster strikes.

DB *The Spanish Civil War also produced a remarkable body of attendant culture, all those wonderful songs, poems by Pablo Neruda, Antonio Machado, Miguel Hernandez and many others. Picasso's "Guernica." Most recently, Ken Loach, a British film director, did a film called* Land and Freedom. *Before that Carlos Saura did one called* Ay, Carmela. *Why do you think the Spanish Civil War has been such a fertile area for artists?*

For one thing because of its complexity. At the time when the left was dominated by the communist movement, there was a simplistic look at the Spanish Civil War. There are the fascists and here is the Popular Front. And that was it. Of course, it was more complicated than that. There were the various elements on the left, including primarily the anarchists. I didn't really know very much about that. I really first learned about that when I read George Orwell's wonderful book *Homage to Catalonia*. He participated in the Spanish Civil War, although I remember that he hesitated at one point to shoot a fascist on the other side because he said the fascist was running across the field and was losing his pants, and he couldn't kill a man who was los-ing his pants. I liked that spirit. He wrote about his experience in Barcelona in the early part of the war, when Barcelona was anarchist territory. The anarchists in Barcelona and in Catalonia, that area, were living in an amazing way. In the midst of the war against Franco, they had created an egalitarian society. Orwell's description of that makes you much more interested in what an anarchist society might be like. But he also talks about the anarchists then being betrayed by the communists, who couldn't stand what the anarchists were doing, who saw them as people who were weakening the fight against fascism. Ken Loach's film *Land and Freedom* dwells very precisely on that point. He has this young man who is a communist but who watches what happens, watches the ugliness of the communist participation in that war, and then learns something by the end of the film.

DB *Let's talk about the American left and its values. We hear these terms, progressive, left. What does it mean to you? What are left values?*

Left values. When I think of left values I think of socialism. To me the word left has such a broad range. They talk about left-liberals. To me the word "left," I want to make it a little more precise, even though socialism itself is not a very precise term. But socialism not in the Soviet sense, not in the bureaucratic sense, not in the Bolshevik sense, but socialism in the sense of Eugene Debs and Mother Jones and Emma Goldman and anarchist socialists. Left values are fundamentally egalitarian values. If I had to say what is at the center of left values, it's the idea that everyone has a fundamental right to the necessary things of life and the good things of life, that there should be no dispropor-tions in the world. It doesn't mean perfect equality, we can't possibly achieve that. I notice that your sweater is better than mine, I'm sorry. But we both have a sweater, which is something. The idea of equality. The principles of the Declaration of Independence, even though it was not written by a leftist—Thomas Jefferson, a leftist?—the idea that everybody has an equal right to life, liberty and the pursuit of happiness, to me is a remarkable statement of left values. It would have to be extended, of course, because in the Declaration of Independence it was all men. It would have to be extended as the fem-inists of 1848 in the U.S. did when they created a new Declaration and added "women" to it, men and women. Then it would have to be extended internationally. One of the crucial values that the left must embrace is a value of international solidarity and equality across national lines. That's very important, because it changes everything if you begin to understand that the lives of children in other countries are equivalent to the lives of children in our country. Then war becomes impossible. I've found it just speaking around the country, presenting what I think are left values. I talk about the equal right of everybody to these things and about extending the principles of the Declaration of Independence all over the world. I find that people everywhere I go, and these are not audiences of only left people, these are assemblies of people, a thousand high school students who are assembled forcibly to hear me, they agree with this. It makes sense. It seems right. It seems moral. They find themselves then accepting what they didn't accept before, for instance that the dropping of the bomb on Hiroshima cannot be properly assessed within the limits of discussion that have generally been set in our society. But if you change those limits by simply introducing the idea that the children of Japan have an equal right to life as the children of the U.S., then suddenly it is impossible to drop a bomb in Hiroshima, just as it would be impossible to drop a bomb on the children of New York, even in order to end World War II faster.

DB   *When you equate Hiroshima with New York, suddenly what was acceptable can be understood in a different light. You've shifted cities to bring home insights elsewhere. In your play,* Marx in Soho—*that's Soho in New York, I believe, not in London—right?*

Marx lived in Soho in London for a good part of his life, a poor district of London. I have Marx explain to the audience in the present that he asked the powers that be to return him to where he lived in Soho, and by bureaucratic error they returned him to Soho, New York, which gives him then an opportunity to talk not just about his life in nineteenth-century Europe and Soho there, but to talk about what he sees around him in New York, in the U.S., on his sudden return.

DB   *And there's an exchange between his wife, Jenny, and Karl that I find very interesting. About the left and revolutionary factions. Would you tell that?*

They have several exchanges. I've taken a few liberties—but then, liberties are not given, they are taken. So I have Jenny call Marx on a number of issues where she feels he's wanting. One of them is what you just talked about, factionalism. Marx was in many ways a lovable person. To put it another way, to certain people he was a lovable person. To his daughter Eleanor he was a very lovable person. To other people, he was really hard to take and could be very nasty. I hate to say this, but sometimes there are people on the left who are nastier to other people on the left than they are to what is called the class enemy. Proudhon, the French anarchist who coined the term "anarchism," became an object of Marx's scorn. Marx could be very arrogant. Proudhon didn't know anything about political economy. For that matter, who knows anything about political economy except Marx? He wrote a very nasty letter to Proudhon. He wrote a book in response to Proudhon's book *The Philosophy of Poverty*, called *The Poverty of Philosophy*. His wife, Jenny, said, Please, why are you doing this? Why does every revolutionary group with five members expel three? They have a number of exchanges. She also argues with him about his writing style and how he's writing about political economy in a way that nobody can understand. She says, Why don't you make it simple? This whole thing about "surplus value." Just say that the workers don't get what they deserve.

DB *What in your view accounts for that tendency toward factionalism and splinterism on the left?*

Desperation, for the same reason that accounts for factionalism among the working class, among the poor, black against white, immigrant against native-born. That is, it's easier to turn against the people closest to you than to take on the big job of crossing over into enemy territory and combating the enemy. So I think that's one important factor in this business of internecine left warfare.

DB *Do you think perhaps also that segments of the left, or people who call themselves progressives, have read reports of their own obituary in the corporate-controlled media and have believed them and act accordingly?*

That's an interesting point. I think it's true. You hear people on the left who tell everybody, Don't believe the media. Then they watch the six o'clock news and come away from it and say, Things are terrible.

There's no left any more. Clinton and Gingrich are in charge. As if there isn't a whole world of potential opposition outside which is not represented on television or in the media. So it's interesting how all of us fall prey to getting absorbed by the major media, no matter how we rail against them.

DB   *The Good Fight is a documentary about the Spanish Civil War, focusing on the American volunteers in the Abraham Lincoln Brigade. You used that in your classes. What was the response?*

People were very moved because they saw young Americans like themselves, including a few black people, a few women, who were outraged by what was happening in Europe and by fascism and leaving everything, sometimes lying to their families about where they were going. I remember showing the film and looking around at my students and seeing students with tears in their eyes, so moved. There's so much talk about young people, college people, being cynical, being the me generation, being conservative. I taught all through the 1980s and the Reagan era, when exactly this kind of description was given to young people, and I found that wasn't true. It becomes a self-fulfilling prophecy. If you believe it's true, then you won't bring up what might awaken students, the fundamental idealism that young people have. Young people want to believe in something good. People everywhere want to believe in something good. But they need to be helped in that. That's what education should be about.

DB   *You had the incident with Jerry Weinberg, your football friend. When I was fourteen or fifteen, in high school in New York, I had a crush on Kerry Allen, a very thin, pale, blonde, completely different from the ethnic background that I had grown up in. She was going to Europe on vacation. Here I was hoping to go to the Catskills. But she was going to Europe. I said, You're going to France, Spain? She said, "I'm not going to Spain. It's a fascist government and Franco is an evil dictator." I was very taken. First of all, I had a crush on her, so I was listening very carefully to her every word. I was deeply impressed by that kind of commitment. It sparked an interest in me to look into what happened in Spain in the 1930s.*

I'm glad you didn't run into a blue-eyed, blonde fascist, or we might not be in the same room today.

DB *What about the idea of equality of opportunity, which is a big theme today, versus equality of condition and then the outcome?*

The conservatives, and sometimes the liberals, make a big thing of, Oh, well, what we just want to give people is equality of opportunity. Which doesn't ensure that people will have equal access to things. We'll give them an education and we'll send them out into the world and see what happens. Basically that's it. We've done our best. We've let you out there. And now let the fittest survive. It's a Darwinian idea. You might say it's a semi-Darwinian idea, since the true Darwinian would say, Start people from birth and put them on their own. They say, No, we'll catch them at eighteen. We'll give them an education, and then we'll set them out on their own. Our values should be that people should have health care and housing and work and food and an education, the fundamental things they need, and that should be guaranteed. Besides, to say we're giving people opportunity and then some people will be able to take advantage of those opportunities and other people will not, that consigns to poverty those people who don't have, let's say, moneymaking skills, moneymaking intelligence. The special kind of qualities that enable some people to become millionaires. These people may be poets or musicians, or they may just be decent people, or they may be carpenters and so on. But they won't have a chance. So it's very important to rid ourselves of the notion that it's sufficient to give people so-called equality of opportunity. Besides, it's very hard to measure what equality of opportunity is and when you really have given people an equal opportunity to do something.

February 5, 1997

DB *The title of your memoir is* You Can't Be Neutral on a Moving Train. *Why did you pick a title like that?*

To confuse people, so that everybody who introduces me at a lecture gets it all wrong, like, You Can't Be Training in a Neutral Place. Actually, the title came out of my classroom teaching, where I would start off my classes explaining to my students from the start, because I didn't want to deceive them, that I would be taking stands on everything. They would hear my point of view in this course, that this would not be a neutral course. My point to them was that in fact it was impossible to be neutral, really, that is, you can't be neutral on a moving train, in the sense that the world is already moving in certain directions. Things are already happening. Wars are taking place. Children are going hungry. In a world like this, already moving in certain, often terrible directions, to be neutral or to stand by is to collaborate with what is happening. I didn't want to be a collaborator, and I didn't want to invite my students to be collaborators.

DB   *I find the structure of the book, the way you laid out the chapters, rather imaginative and artistic. Usually autobiographical details come right in front: I was born in...My parents were..., etc. You give that toward the end. What did you have in mind?*

I felt that if I started off, as so many of these things do, with, My grandmother came from...then people would immediately go to sleep. When I start somebody's autobiography like that, I usually skip, I want to immediately get to the person. I'm sorry. I like your grandmother and your grandfather. Nothing against them. But please: you, you. So I decided to plunge right into what I thought was a very important part of my life, my time in the South and then only towards the end give the reader some sense of where I came from and what my upbringing was, a kind of suspense story, implying of course that I'm keeping the reader in suspense.

DB   *In that chapter toward the end of the book, "Growing Up Class-Conscious," you write of an incident in Times Square. You were living in Brooklyn at the time. It not only gave you a lump on the side of your head, but it also had a big political impact on you. Can you describe that?*

A lump on the side of the head. Very often you ask people, What turned you around politically? What made you politically active? What converted you from a liberal to a radical, or from A to B? Very often it's very hard to trace. But sometimes there's actually an identifiable precipitating incident. There was in my case. I was a seventeen-year-old kid living in the slums of Brooklyn. There living on the same block were these young communists who were older than I and seemed very politically sophisticated. They asked me to come to a demonstration at Times Square. I had never been to a demonstration, and going to Times Square sounded very exciting. I went along. There was Times Square. It seemed like nothing was going on except the usual crowds at Times Square. But my friend said, Wait. Ten o'clock. Ten o'clock appeared on the *New York Times* building, which flashes the time. Suddenly, banners were unfurled all around me. People started marching down the street. It was very exciting. I wasn't even sure what it was all about, except that vaguely I thought that it was against war. They seemed to be for good causes. I went along. At some point there were these two women in front of us carrying banners. This was before the age of feminist consciousness, even among leftists. My friends said, We mustn't let these two women carry this banner. You take one end. I'll take the other end. It was like Charlie Chaplin, picking up that red flag, a railroad signal flag and suddenly looking and there's this army of unemployed marching behind him in this demonstration. Then suddenly, holding these banners, marching along with the crowd, I heard these sirens. I thought, There must be a fire somewhere around. But no. Soon the mounted police, driving their horses into the crowd, beating the people. It was a wild scene. Before I knew it I was spun around by the shoulder, hit and knocked unconscious. I woke up, I don't know how much later, in a doorway. Times Square was back as it was before. It was very eerie, as if nothing had happened. My friend was gone. The demonstration was over. The police were gone. As you suggested, I was not only nursing a hurt head, but hurt feelings about our country. All the things these radicals had been saying about the state is not neutral, the forces of government are not neutral as between the rich and the poor, but on the side of the powerful. There really is no freedom of speech in this country if you're a radical. That was brought home to me, because these people were engaging in nonviolent peaceful demonstration, presumably protected by the Constitution, and zoom! the police are there beating heads and breaking up the demonstration.

DB *And shortly after that, or a few years later, you got a job in the Brooklyn Navy Yard. You were involved in organizing the apprentices into the union.*

There were actually four of us, four young guys who had become apprentices. I was a ship fitter. Another guy was a machinist. Another guy was a sheet metal worker. Another guy was a joiner. We were not allowed into the AFL craft unions. The unskilled workers in the ship-yard, and many of them were black chippers and burners and riveters, doing the dirtiest, toughest work, were not allowed into the unions. We decided to organize the young workers, the apprentices, into a union, which we set about to do. It was a wonderful experience.

DB *I asked that to bring us to what's going on today with unions. I confess to doing the* New York Times *crossword puzzle almost every day. I hope you don't think less of me. The other day there was a clue: "picket line pariah." Four letters. The answer, of course, was "scab." This term "scab," at least for your generation, carried a tremendous stigma. It was fightin' words. A tremendous amount of shame was attendant to that. But today, with the growth of what are called "replacement workers" and "temporary workers," things have changed rather dramatically.*

Unquestionably. In the 1930s and 1940s there was tremendous trade union consciousness coming out of the Depression and even continuing through the war. So that the word "scab" meant some-thing. Crossing a picket line was something that you just didn't do. It was morally unacceptable. Today, in fact just the other day, my wife and I were passing Dunkin' Donuts in our neighborhood. You talked about a confession. This is my turn to confess. I love Dunkin' Donuts. There were three pickets in front of Dunkin' Donuts, members of the carpenters' union. We stopped to take their leaflets and to talk to them. I always do that with people on the picket line so they won't feel alone, so they feel they have some support. They were protesting the fact that Dunkin' Donuts had constructed this new Dunkin' Donuts shop with non-union labor. But a lot of people were going past them into Dunkin' Donuts. Some people were not, but a lot of people were. There's no doubt that today there's a much weakened sense of trade union solidarity. The hope is that it is beginning to change, that the labor movement has reached its low point, as it did with the AFL in the 1920s, and just as there was a resurgence in the early 1930s with the CIO that perhaps we're on the verge of a new wave of union mili-tancy. There's a new consciousness of organizing service workers— we've become more of a service economy than a manufacturing econo-my—and organizing non-skilled workers comparable to the CIO, which organized all those people on the assembly line who were not being taken into AFL unions. So now there are maids and waiters and hotel and restaurant employees and clerks, there are all these organiz-ing drives among technical and staff workers at universities. John Sweeney, who comes right out of the Service Employees International, is now head of the AFL, so there are signs of new rank and file move-ments, with the Teamsters and the miners and so on. We cannot have a transformation of American society without a new labor movement.

DB *Michael Moore, the filmmaker and producer of TV Nation, says when Reagan broke the air traffic controllers union in 1981, that we all should have refused to fly, and we didn't. In that we were complicit.*

Of course he's absolutely right. The fact that we were not ready to do that is a sign of how dispirited was the union movement and the left at that time. It didn't even occur to the trade union movement in the country that they might carry on a national campaign to support these people who were fired by Reagan. Of course that would have been the thing to do.

DB *The state of unions and organized labor in the U.S. contrasts rather sharply with the situation in Europe, where there's enormous resis-tance to the neo-liberal agenda in Germany, France and Italy.*

One of the consequences in Europe of having a much stronger labor movement than we have here is that they have much, much stronger social programs than ours. There's a dramatic difference between what these countries in Western Europe with strong trade unions do for the poor, the old people, unemployed people, women and what we do. If you are unemployed in this country, you get unem-ployment compensation, which is a small part of what a minimum wage really would be. It only lasts for a certain amount of time. In European countries, what you get may be very close to what you were getting. You may get 80%. I was just talking to a couple from Norway who were visiting here. Unemployed in Norway? You get 80% of what you were getting in your salary, and it lasts for a long time, until you get another job. It isn't cut off. Our unemployment is cut off. Same with other things. Their social security, old age pensions, are much more generous than ours. Their care for women who are working and who are pregnant, these women get long periods of time to take care of their kids at full pay. Remember how Clinton felt he was being very generous when he suggested that women should get time off from work when they get pregnant without being punished, but without pay. So in order to begin to take care of our people in the way that people are taken care of in Western Europe, with their health program and so on, we would need a strong labor movement and a strong consumer movement for all those people who are not members of trade unions but who are supporters of trade unions. Going back to what you said about Michael Moore and his suggestion that we should not have taken air travel in order to support the flight controllers, the boycott is a very powerful weapon. Cesar Chavez and the farm workers showed that. They managed to organize a national boycott of grapes and had a tremendous effect.

DB *Clinton's first Secretary of Labor, Robert Reich, who is now teaching at Brandeis, said that, "The jury is still out on whether the traditional union is still necessary for the new workplace." And the late Commerce Secretary Ron Brown observed, "Unions are OK where they are. Where they are not, it is not clear what sort of organization should represent workers."*

I suppose Brown thought that the National Association of Manufacturers would be better suited to represent workers. I'm disappointed in what Robert Reich had to say about not being sure about the function of unions. He should know better. But here are two members of the Clinton Administration, and I suppose they represent the thinking of the Clinton Administration on the importance of unions. That change of perspective is not going to come naturally out of this administration or any administration. It's going to come out of the pressure exerted from below, strikes and organizing of labor.

DB *That speaks to that famous comment by Frederick Douglass that power concedes nothing without demand.*

That's right. That wonderful statement of Douglass that he made a few years before the Civil War. It represented at that time the view of the abolitionists that they could not depend on the national government to do away with slavery. The anti-slavery movement grew and grew because it was needed in the face of a national government that collaborated with slavery, including even Lincoln, who was so reluctant to do anything about ending slavery and who had to be pushed by a very powerful abolitionist movement of black and white abolitionists. Frederick Douglass was very conscious of the fact that you had to build power from below in order to get any kind of change in society.

DB *In October 1996, in Everett near Boston, you were involved in an action at the Richmark Curtain Factory. What were the circumstances?*

I really didn't know what was happening at the Richmark Curtain Factory. My ignorance was typical of the ignorance of most people about the working conditions of people in their own community. We very often do not know what is happening within a mile of us, where people are working under terrible conditions for very low and miserable wages. Elaine Bernard, head of the Harvard Trade Union Program, who seems to know what is going on everywhere, called me. She's the kind of person who, when she calls you, you must listen. When she tells you to be somewhere at eight o'clock in the morning, you must be there. I don't know what punishment would be meted out to you if you didn't. It's left very vague. So you respond. She told me about what was happening. The Richmark Curtain Company in Everett, north of Boston, was hiring these mostly women immigrants from El Salvador who were working under terrible conditions. They couldn't spend more than three minutes in the bathroom or their pay would be docked. They were given work to take home and being paid according to how much work they did, but the pay amounted to less than the minimum wage. An organizing attempt began by UNITE, which is this new trade union formed by the Amalgamated Clothing Workers and the International Ladies Garment Workers Union. They began to organize the workers at Richmark. More than half of them signed cards saying they wanted a union to represent them. Whereupon ten of the workers were fired. So a rally was going to take place at Richmark to support these workers, to demand that the workers' jobs be restored, that the Richmark Company recognize the union. I came down to the rally. It so happened that John Sweeney was in town. Elaine Bernard got in touch with him. And apparently he reacted to her the way most people do: he couldn't say no. He came down and spoke at the rally. There was a great turnout of community support, people from other unions. Thirteen of us went into the plant to talk to the CEO of Richmark and ask him to reinstate the workers and recognize the union. He refused flatly on everything. We said we wouldn't leave until there was some kind of recognition. He called the police. The police came. The police chief of Everett himself came. He apparently hadn't confronted a situation like this before. He was a little apologetic. He apologized that he didn't have enough handcuffs to go around. So we were all arrested. We spent a day in the lockup. A trial date was set. But, remarkably, just shortly after that I was going out of town for a speaking thing. I called my wife and she said, Well, the Richmark Company seems to have caved in. They're willing to talk to the union. Since then, there has been—in fact, you told me this. (People who interview you are not supposed to know more than the interviewee. You're supposed to get your information from me. But you're the one who told me.) Just the other day Richmark Company agreed to a contract and dropped the charges against us. They drew up a contract with the union. It was a remarkable victory. To me it was a sign of what is possible when there's real solidarity, when community organizations, other trade unions all get together to support a small group of people who would be helpless by themselves. But that's the old idea of trade unionism, solidarity, the idea of the IWW, that radical union of the beginning of the twentieth century: An injury to one is an injury to all.

DB *You've often used literature to exemplify things in your books and your public talks. You've mentioned reading Upton Sinclair's* The Jungle, *John Steinbeck's* The Grapes of Wrath, *when you were young and being influenced by them, and most of all, by Charles Dickens. There's a segment from* Hard Times *that you often use in your public lectures. Why do you use Dickens and* Hard Times?

Dickens was a class-conscious writer. It's interesting. He was a contemporary of Karl Marx, two different ends of the spectrum. Not different ends of the political spectrum, but of the tactical spectrum. Marx was writing political economy. Dickens was writing novels. But Marx was talking about class and class consciousness and doing analysis, and Dickens was representing the lives of the poor in writing *Oliver Twist* and *David Copperfield* and *Great Expectations* and *Hard Times*. Dickens did not have the advanced social consciousness of Marx in seeing the possibility of collective action to change things. But he had many important insights. In *Hard Times*, you were pointing to the fact that—actually it was only once in one of my talks recently that I referred to *Hard Times*, but now I'm going to do it again, now that you've provoked me. I was trying to make a point to the audience that all of these descriptions of our economic situation which are presented in grand, sweeping terms fail to focus on reality. Take statistics. The income of Americans grew last year. Did your income grow last year? Did the income of these people who are working in restaurants or in factories grow last year? So we get these large statements made about the economy, saying, The economy is up. The economy is down. Whose economy? For whom? Whose income grew? A class-conscious person asks the question, whenever presented with an overall statistic, what Kurt Vonnegut called a "granfalloon" in one of his books, which is sort of a great balloon which needs to be punctured in order to get to the reality of things. In *Hard Times*, Dickens has a scene which to me clarifies what is going on. He has this caricature, I hope it's a caricature, of a professor who believes in facts and statistics. In his class he has a working-class girl who listens to him. He is saying, Students, England is a very prosperous country, isn't it? Look at all the wealth that England has. And aren't we all therefore prosperous? This working-class girl is shy, but this somehow strikes her in a certain way, this Sissy Jupe. She says, I'm not sure if we're prosperous because England is prosperous. If England has all this money, I'd like to know, how much of it is ours? That's a question that should be asked today of all the statistics. My father, who was an uneducated man and probably did not know what the word "statistics" meant, he would...

DB   *Even if he wrecked his brains to find out?*

That was one of my mother's English-as-a-second-language statements. I wrecked my brains to try to figure this out and I couldn't do it. But my father was responding to this confident cliché: Figures don't lie. His response was, Figures don't lie, but liars figure. Statistics. The Dow Jones average is an example. It's supposed to register how our country is doing, how the stock market is doing. Does the stock market register how ordinary people are living when fifty percent of all stock is held by one percent of the population? The Dow Jones average is going up, up, up and the wages of ordinary people are going down in real terms, in the last fifteen years. The Dow Jones average has gone up four hundred percent, and the wages of eighty percent of the population have gone down fifteen percent. So to me it is very important in teaching to prepare young people to look at statistics and look at these granfalloons, these overall statements about the economy and the country with great skepticism.

DB   *Could you read that section from* Hard Times?

Sissy Jupe is describing this to Gradgrind's daughter, who's also a little skeptical of her father, and who has befriended Sissy Jupe, this working-class girl. She's describing to her the class that she was in, Gradgrind's.

"And he said, In this nation there are fifty millions of money. Isn't this a prosperous nation, and aren't you in a thriving state? I said I didn't know. I thought I couldn't know whether it was a prosperous nation or not or whether I was in a thriving state or not unless I knew who had got the money and whether any of it was mine." Louisa, Gradgrind's daughter, herself gets involved in a conflict with her father over his tendency to put everything in general and statistical terms and to lose sight of the human consequences of these statistics. He's pushing Louisa into a marriage with somebody properly named Bounderby. Dickens loves those names. This is horrifying to her. She says, "Father, I've often thought, life is very short." Gradgrind says, "Still, the average duration of human life has proved to have increased of late years. The calculations of various life assurance offices have established that fact." Louisa says, "I speak of my own life, Father." Dickens to me was always a wonderful source of insight into reality.

DB   *Speaking about education and your years as a teacher, what were the qualities you were looking for in your students?*

Maybe you should put it this way: What were the qualities I was hoping would develop in my students? I suppose the most important single thing I wanted to develop in my students was a determination to look into things on their own, to not accept authority, including my own authority, to challenge me. I challenged them constantly to challenge me in class, to go and look up the things that I was talking about and bring in countervailing views. I insisted that all issues were controversial, that they couldn't believe books, that the fact that something was in a book or newspaper didn't give it the certainty of truth. They had to check up on things and investigate things for themselves because our sources of information are skewed in the direction favored by those people who control the media, the book publishing industry, who for that matter control the educational system. So that was one of the most important things I wanted my students to learn. Maybe another thing I wanted them to learn was that education does not come simply through classrooms, books, degrees, teaching, that they could learn most about the world by getting outside the classroom and encountering what was happening to real people in the world outside. That's why instead of giving exams to my students, testing them, as if testing is more important than learning, I would say, Look, your job for the semester—this was in a course I gave called "Law and Justice in America" and in which I had 400 students signed up every year—is to go out into the community and to find a group that you would like to work with, a group that is interested in something you are interested in. Work with that group, a group that is in some way connected with issues of law and justice. Just work with that group. I'm not going to tell you what group. If you want to join the Young Republicans and see what they're like, OK. Of course, not too many of my students did. Some of them joined Amnesty International. Some of them worked with Mobilization for Survival, or with groups that were raising bail for prisoners. Or they formed their own groups. Some of my students formed a group that investigated the legal problems of veterans who were the victims of Agent Orange in the Vietnam War defoliation campaign. Other students produced a handbook for tenants to protect them against landlords. So the idea was for the students to learn about law and justice by encountering real life problems.

DB *Do you miss teaching and the students?*

I miss the classroom and the encounter with students and getting to know them. But I'm not completely divorced from that situation, because now that I'm not teaching in a formal way I do go around the country and speak to groups of young people and community people, so I have the opportunity to have an interchange, to do a kind of teaching. A week ago I spoke to Philips Exeter Academy, which is a prep school in New Hampshire. There were a thousand students, a captive audience, as high school students very often are when they are assembled in the morning and told, You must come. I don't mind captive audiences. I figure, OK, I'll imprison them for an hour. That's OK. But I had an opportunity to talk to a thousand high school students. It happened to be Inauguration Day. It happened also to be the day for celebrating Martin Luther King's birthday. I was able to talk to them about what the two represented, about the shallow politics of presidential inaugurations and what that represented and the meaningful politics of social protest represented by King. I speak to community colleges, to high schools. I love to speak to high school students. And to community groups. As a result I don't miss teaching as much as I might have if I simply retired from teaching and played tennis.

DB *John Silber is the former president of Boston University and now its Chancellor. You worked for him for many years. He was your boss, so to speak.*

He thought he was my boss.

DB *Now he is Governor William Weld's education czar for the state of Massachusetts. The New York Times did a profile of Silber a little while ago. I'd like you to comment on what he says. He insists that there is a "natural aristocracy of intelligence and reason" and argues that American universities are not supposed to be democratic institutions. Then he gives this example. "The hospital is not a democracy. You mean when we come into the operating theater, the surgeon is supposed to ask the nurses, What do you think I ought to do next? How many are in favor of making the incision here? No, the decision is made on the basis of the exalted competence of the surgeon. You don't go out in the hall and say, Let's get a couple of janitors and see what they think about it."*

That's typical John Silber. He loves to use analogies that are absurd. Of course, he has declared himself as a surgeon in the operating room. What's interesting to me is that he considers the student body literally as a body to be cut up by an expert. I guess you might say, Yes, he is an expert at cutting up the student body. But to assume that the president of a college is in the same position with regard to education that a surgeon is with regard to medicine is an absurd statement. In fact, the university president does not know as much as faculty, and very often does not know as much as students do about education, what kind of education they should be getting. As Silber himself said, he doesn't believe in democracy in education. If education is not democratic, then it is teaching students that democracy is not desirable. So are you going to teach young people to take their place in a democratic society by first putting them through four years of an anti-democratic institution? Education, if it is going to prepare students to create a democracy outside, should be in itself democratic.

DB   *Some years ago, speaking to a gathering of university presidents on the West Coast, Silber talked darkly about those teachers who "poison the well of academe." His two chief examples? Noam Chomsky and Howard Zinn. Tell me about this "well."*

I guess Silber thinks that there is some kind of pure well. That pure well is education, the body of knowledge as it has been, and then along come people like Chomsky and me and we are ruining it. Actually, that is the kind of accusation that is now being made in a larger sense about education by the right wing in this country, who claim that education was wonderful before the multiculturalists came in, before we had feminist studies and black studies and Native American studies and Chicano studies. The well was pure before students had to read the *Autobiography of Malcolm X* alongside Thomas Hardy, before they were given *I, Rigoberta Menchú*, the autobiography of a Guatemalan servant girl and rebel, alongside of Tolstoy and Rousseau. There's this pure well that existed before and now all these other influences are coming in, influences which started with the movements of the 1960s. So of course it was not a very pure well. It was pure only in the sense of the racial purity that was so talked about during the fascist years. A well that I would argue was itself poisonous in the sense that it perpetuated an education that left out large numbers of the world's people.

DB   *Literature isn't your only source of understanding the world. You've said that looking at bumper stickers is one of your principal forms of research. You saw one that said, "If God had intended us to vote, he would have given us candidates."*

Right. In talking to audiences I changed it a little because I was a little bothered by it. I took the liberty of editing the bumper sticker, which is a terrible thing to do to a scholarly statement. I changed it to, "If the gods had intended us to vote, they would have given us candidates." It was a flippant way of pointing to the inadequacy of voting as a way of bringing about social change. I try in my classes and in my talks to divest my listeners of the notion which is thrown at us from the time we get into school and start taking civics classes that going into a voting booth every two or four years is the ultimate act of citizenship. The implication is that all you have to do is vote and then your leaders will take care of everything for you. History is very, very clear on the inadequacy of voting in bringing about social change. What we learn from history is that whenever anything important had to be done, whenever any serious injustice had to be rectified, you could not depend on the government, on the political system, on the Constitution, on the Bill of Rights, on any of those formal mechanisms. The so-called channels that you are always asked to go through are not channels but mazes into which you are invited to get lost. What people have had to do historically is to go outside those channels. The anti-slavery movement did it. They couldn't depend on Lincoln and Congress. A hundred years later they couldn't depend on Kennedy and Johnson to do away with racial segregation in the South. The labor movement could not depend on any of the formal mechanisms of government. They had to go out on strike and get beaten and killed and face the National Guard and the army. Women could not depend on anything in the Constitution or that came out of Washington. They had to form their own movement.

DB *The 1996 elections were rather striking in the turnout, particularly. It was 49%, the lowest since 1924. What do you attribute that to? Is it apathy, disgust, people fed up? What's your sense of that?*

There's a long record of studies of people who don't vote. It's very clear that the people who don't vote are largely the people at the lower income levels. The reason they don't vote is they do not see that either of the candidates, either of the major parties, have solutions to their condition. Their condition is rooted in something much deeper than what can be remedied by a new President or a different party coming into office. In this last election the turnout was even lower than in other elections and Clinton, in barely winning, was given the vote of approval by something like 22% of the eligible voting population. That's been the pattern. Reagan was winning what were called overwhelming victories, that was a media statement. Actually, he was getting 29, 30, 31% of the eligible electorate voting for him. The indifference to voting, the unenthusiasm in voting is the result of alienation from the political system and a recognition that neither major party has solutions to the problems that most people face.

DB   *The Alliance had its founding convention in Texas, outside of San Antonio, in November. This is a new political formation. You were there. What was going on?*

I wasn't there for the whole thing. But I was there for a day or so. What happened in Texas at that founding convention for the Alliance, I think now it's called the Alliance for Democracy, was an attempt to initiate a new populist movement. That it was held in Texas was a sign of that, because all the populist movements of the 1880s and 1890s really had Texas as an important beginning source of activity. It's an attempt to organize people around the country outside of the two major parties, around issues of class, economic issues, recognizing that corporate control of the economy, of politics, of the media is ruining our country. So that which started in Texas at the founding meeting of the Alliance is still going on. That is, groups around the country are organizing, are keeping in touch with one another. I get these mysterious messages on the Internet which tell me that chapters of the Alliance are forming around the country. The hope is that these various attempts that are going on today at forming new populist groups, that is, the New Party, the Labor Party, the Alliance, that all of these at some point will begin to get together, the trade union movement, the National Organization for Women, and that they will create a new movement for social change.

DB   *Let's close with two of your favorite poems. One is from A* People's History of the United States. *You quote Langston Hughes, "Let America Be America Again."*

Langston Hughes wrote this in the mid-1930s

...I am the poor white, fooled and pushed apart,
I am the Negro bearing slavery's scars.
I am the red man driven from the land,
I am the immigrant clutching the hope I seek—

And finding only the same old stupid plan.
Of dog eat dog, of mighty crush the weak....

O, let America be America again—
The land that never has been yet—
And yet must be—the land where every man is free.
The land that's mine—the poor man's, Indian's, Negro's

ME—

Who made America,
Whose sweat and blood, whose faith and pain,
Whose hand at the foundry, whose plow in the rain,
Must bring back our mighty dream again.

Sure, call me any ugly name you choose—
The steel of freedom does not stain.
From those who live like leeches on the people's lives,
We must take back our land again,
America!...

DB *And in* You Can't Be Neutral on a Moving Train *in the last chapter, "The Possibility of Hope," you have a poem by Alice Walker, perhaps best known for* The Color Purple, *but who was also your student at Spelman College.*

Yes, I love Alice Walker's poems, this one particularly, which is called "Once." It's from her first book of poems.

It is true—
I've always loved
the daring
ones
Like the black young
man
Who tried

to crash
All barriers
at once,
wanted to
swim
At a white
beach (in Alabama)
Nude.

DB   *August 24, 1997. Someone's going to be 75 years old.*

Why did you bring that up?

DB   *I think it's a cause for great celebration. I was wondering, What about the next 75 years? What are your plans?*

My plan is to not do anything but be interviewed by you. I'm tired of going around talking to other people. If I just sit around and talk to you and you send it out on satellite, it will save me a lot of trouble.

DB   *I think I speak for a lot of people around the country and around the world who really appreciate your efforts and your steadfastness and determination to make a difference. Thanks a lot and happy birthday.*

Thank you.

LaGuardia, Upton Sinclair, and the Death Penalty

October 4, 1997

DB *Congratulations on* The Zinn Reader, *not to say a book, but a mighty tome of 668 pages. How did this come about?*

I resent that, the tone in talking about the tome. How did it come about? I swear it's not my fault, all those pages. It takes two people to carry this book across the room. But think of the contents. How did it happen? It was the idea of the editor. I always blame other people for these things. Seven Stories Press is an independent publisher in New York. The editor is Dan Simon. I met him in Paris. I always like to point to meetings in Paris as the starting point to big things. At that time he was working in a little one-table restaurant called Le Petit Vatel. We became friends. Years later, he turns up somehow as the editor of this ingenious little press and says, We should collect your writings. So I sent him a whole bunch of things, stuff from my out-of-print books from the civil rights days, from the Vietnam days, op-ed pieces I'd written for the *Boston Globe* and various what they call "fugitive essays" in which you run away from everybody. I said, Pick what you want. He wrote back and said, I want it all. The result is this, as you say, tome. It has my very first article that I wrote for *Harper's.* It has pieces I wrote from the South for *The Nation.* It has stuff from my book on SNCC. That's only in the section on race. *The Reader* also has sections on class, war, law, history, means and ends. We divided my writings up into all of these things.

DB *Actually, I wanted to ask you about your days playing with the legendary New York Giants baseball stars like Bill Terry, Carl Hubbell and Mel Ott. What was that like for you, playing with those great Hall of Famers?*

It's not easy being in the shadow of such giants, you know. To be a pygmy on the Giant baseball team is no fun. I enjoyed it, I must say.

DB   *Did you ever go to the Polo Grounds to watch them play?*

Of course I went to the Polo Grounds. But I went more often to Ebbets Field, which was geographically closer. I didn't own the high-speed auto which I have now, at that time. I was fourteen. Ebbets Field was closer. So I'd wait until the Giants came to play the Dodgers. It was always a wonderful moment for cruelty to the Dodgers and for cruel gibes at my Dodger fan friends. Also, Ebbets Field had a nice, short, right-field wall which was perfect for Mel Ott. He lifted that right foot. He had that special thing that he lifted his right foot, I don't know how he did it, and hit the ball over the right field wall again and again. Those were good days.

DB   *Are you following sports at all today, where teams are moving around like checkers?*

It's very hard for me to follow it. I'm stuck in the old days where there was simply a National League and an American League. There weren't divisions. I knew the names of the teams. The Dodgers were still in Brooklyn and Boston had the Braves. Cincinnati had the Reds, although I think during the McCarthy period they changed it to the Redlegs. So it's hard for me to keep up these days.

DB   *Are you following the political economy of sports today, where a team is playing off one city or state against another? In football, for example, the Oakland Raiders move to Los Angeles and then back to Oakland again. The Houston Oilers move to Tennessee and the Cleveland Browns move to Baltimore and that kind of thing.*

That's called the free market. It's a wonderful thing.

DB   *But it's not working according to traditional free market dictums, because they're demanding public subsidies from cities and states.*

That means it *is* working according to traditional free market dictums. They've always called it a "free market," but they've always wanted government subsidies.

DB *One person you have focused on, in fact the subject of your first book, was the famous* Little Flower, *Fiorello LaGuardia. I was interested to read in your essay, and here's where I make the connection with sports because LaGuardia talked about "baseball slavery" and demanding its end and asking that the ballplayers become unionized. Rather radical.*

He was way ahead of his time on so many things. I wrote about him before he became Mayor of New York, as a Congressman representing East Harlem in the 1920s. It was presumably the Jazz Age and the age of prosperity and everybody in the country was supposed to be out in the streets dancing the Charleston. But in fact, reading the letters that LaGuardia's constituents wrote to him from East Harlem, it was very clear that this was not an age of prosperity for everybody. In fact, it was so much like our time today, where you hear Clinton going on the air and proclaiming that the economy is in wonderful shape and he cites the statistics. They did exactly the same thing in the twenties because the same thing was happening. The stock market was way, way up, and people's wages were going down. Although the unemployment figures will show that there wasn't a lot of unemployment, there was enough unemployment to make life miserable for a fair number of people. His constituents would write to him and say, My husband is out of work. My kids are hungry. They just turned off the gas because we can't pay our bills. I was interested in reproducing his experience for the reasons of this book because I think it speaks to the situation today.

DB *In your introduction it sounds like you were wandering the streets looking for a dissertation topic and you stumbled upon it.*

That doesn't sound like a really focused scholar, does it? Somebody who wanders the streets looking for a dissertation topic? I was not wandering the streets looking for a dissertation topic. Those are two separate things. One, I was looking for a topic. Two, I was wandering the streets. But I stumbled on a dissertation topic while wandering. I was walking in downtown Manhattan and I passed a decrepit old building which was the municipal archives. The word "archives" always causes a little extra beat of the heart to a true historian. I went in and walked up the stairs and there's this enormous warehouse kind of floor. There was a woman at the desk. What do you have here, I asked. She said, It so happens that Mrs. LaGuardia has just deposited the LaGuardia papers here. I'd been having trouble with a dissertation topic because the topics that I wanted turned out to be dead ends. I wanted to do something on Big Bill Haywood, the great leader of the IWW. It turned out that the Justice Department had confiscated his papers and at a certain point burned them. This is something you wouldn't expect from our upstanding Justice Department, to burn the papers of a radical. They would keep them and hound his grandchildren with them if they were smart. So this leads me to looking for a topic. She said, There are hundreds of filing cabinets dealing with LaGuardia's mayoralty years. In this corner there's a much smaller number of filing cabinets dealing with his Congressional career. That's where I went. Looking through it, I didn't know anything about his Congressional career. But as I began looking through these documents and reading the speeches that he gave in the House of Representatives in the 1920s, I realized that he was a quite extraordinary radical in Congress. Here he was, a Socialist running as a Republican. In fact, one year he ran on both the Republican and Socialist tickets. He opposed the dispatch of Marines to Nicaragua by Coolidge in 1926. He spoke up for the poor.

DB *That dissertation won an award named after Albert Beveridge. What distinguished Albert Beveridge, for people who don't know his name?*

You're trying to embarrass me again. My award was named after Albert Beveridge. He was the leading imperialist in the U.S. Senate in the early part of the twentieth century. When McKinley was trying to decide whether the U.S. should take the Philippines and some people said, We shouldn't do it because so far we've only taken territories contiguous to us, Beveridge said, The Philippines not contiguous to us? Our Navy will make them contiguous. My hero, Albert Beveridge. But what could I do? I'm trying to think of a prize whose name will deter me from taking a prize. There probably are such, but I confess. I compromised and took the prize.

DB *Your dissertation was turned into a book,* LaGuardia in Congress. *Your essay, "LaGuardia in the Jazz Age," appears in* The Zinn Reader. *I sort of only knew him as a mayor, and particularly the fact that he read the comics on the radio during the newspaper strike in New York. To read about his parents in particular was interesting. His father, for example.*

His father was a musician. He was an arranger, a musician and an accompanist for Adelina Patti, a great opera singer of the time. That musicality somehow was taken into LaGuardia's persona. He played clarinet and always loved music and bands. His mother was Jewish. A lot of people didn't know this.

DB *Also from Italy, from Trieste.*

That's right. There were a few Jews in Italy. Her name was Irene Coen-Lazzotti. There were rabbis in her background. LaGuardia's Jewishness is interesting. He not only spoke Yiddish, but six other languages. He was wonderful at languages. In fact, he worked for a while at the Immigration Service of the U.S. He translated for many different people from Europe. At one time during one of his Congressional campaigns he ran against a Jewish candidate. His name was Herman Frank. There were a fair number of Jewish constituents in his district. The race was getting very close. Frank became very desperate. He put out a leaflet in the last days of the campaign accusing LaGuardia of being an anti-Semite, thinking he would get a nice number of Jewish votes that way. LaGuardia responded with his own leaflet, challenging his opponent to a debate on the issues of the campaign, to be conducted entirely in Yiddish. LaGuardia knew very well that Frank, Jewish, did not speak a word of Yiddish. LaGuardia won. He was a character.

DB *He also said of his opponent, Is he looking for a job as a schamas, or does he want to be an elected Congressman? What's a schamas?*

A schamas is the guy that cleans up in the synagogue.

DB *There's a lot of the Jazz Age that does resonate today, particularly the nativism, the anti-immigrant feeling that LaGuardia fought against.*

The 1920s was a field day for anti-immigrant people. They passed restrictive immigration laws which discriminated against people from Southern and Eastern Europe and welcomed people from England, Ireland, Scotland and northern Europe. LaGuardia fought bitterly against that immigration restriction. First of all, being the son of immigrants himself, and second, working with immigrants as an immigration officer, he had a great feeling for people coming to this country.

Probably nobody in the 1920s in Congress spoke as often on the floor of the House of Representatives as LaGuardia did. He was a great speaker.

DB *And during that period, again to see the resonance and echo today, Andrew Mellon, the Secretary of the Treasury, advocated and secured tax cuts for the rich, which LaGuardia opposed.*

The Mellon plan was interesting. You appoint a Secretary of the Treasury, one of the richest men in America, because you know he'll take care of the Treasury, and also take good care of his own treasury. Mellon himself personally stood to gain from lowering the tax rate on the very rich, and that's exactly what he did. Mellon did what we have done in this country in the last fifteen years and even before as we have progressively done away with the progressive income tax by moving it down from what was 85% and 90% at the end of World War II gradually down to 70%, 60% on the upper levels, and finally to 32%, 33%. It was considered a bold act for President Clinton to move it up from 32% to 34%. But the tax rates of today are really even more egregious and more horrible for the poor than the tax rates of the Mellon years. During the Mellon years at least the tax rates on the poor were very low, but today the tax rates on ordinary people are very hard to endure. You can understand why people would respond quickly to politicians who promise to lower taxes. Except that when politicians promise to lower taxes, they never say for whom they will lower them. They've been lowering the taxes a lot on the rich, and not very much on ordinary people.

DB *Back to LaGuardia's father. He joined the American Army in 1898 as a bandmaster. What happened to him?*

You mean in the Army?

DB *There was the case of contaminated meat.*

The Spanish-American War. This is one of the horrible incidents that LaGuardia never could forget. Most people did not know that the casualties the U.S. suffered in the Spanish-American War in 1898, which was called a "splendid little war" by one of our leaders, were mostly not from the battlefield. There were only three months of combat and the battlefield casualties were in the hundreds. But the total casualties were in the thousands, and most of those came from contaminated meat which had been sold to the Army by the packing houses of Chicago. The profit motive operating again and again. We don't care what happens to the people who eat this meat. We're going to make a lot of money selling this contaminated meat to the military. LaGuardia's father was one of those victims.

DB *Would you say that after he became Mayor of New York that that radicalism was tempered?*

Unquestionably. Part of it has to do with I think a very common fact in politics. That is that when you gain executive power and when you're in charge of a situation, you become less free. The forces acting on you understand your power and become more demanding. The business interests and the police interests. As Mayor of New York, LaGuardia became in a number of instances anti-union. I of course admired LaGuardia so much in his Congressional years, but one of the things I remember from his mayoralty career was the Harlem Riot. It started, as riots very often do, with some small incident which becomes magnified. The black people of Harlem went wild through the streets thinking that one of their number had been murdered. Actually he wasn't. But people were on the edge of rebellion. It was 1935, the Depression. Not only was the whole nation suffering, but black people in the ghetto were suffering much, much harder than anybody else. Unemployment rates in Harlem were horrendous. People were living under the most terrible conditions, just ready for an explosion. It exploded in 1935 in what was called the Harlem Riot. LaGuardia appointed a commission to investigate the riot. The research director of the commission was Franklin Frazier, a great African American sociologist and quite radical. Instead of just concentrating on the immediate events of the riot, Franklin Frazier's report insisted on going into the socio-economic roots of the problem. It talked about job discrimination against blacks by the city and by employers who contracted with the city. It talked about the huge gap between the number of people employed by the subway system and the tiny number of blacks employed there. It ended up recommending that the Mayor immediately do away with job discrimination for the city employees and refuse to do a contract with any company that discriminated against black people. LaGuardia suppressed the report. He wouldn't allow the report to be publicized. But finally, it was leaked through the *Amsterdam News*, a black newspaper in Harlem. That was a shameful moment for LaGuardia, I think.

DB *You conclude your essay "Growing Up Class Conscious," which is reprinted in* The Reader, *with climbing up a mountain in New Hampshire. You took some lesson from that.*

I was climbing a mountain in New Hampshire with somebody I had recently met and recently hired. I've actually never hired anybody in my life except for that moment when I was chair of the History Department at Spelman College and had this enormous power to hire one person. I hired Staughton Lynd, a white historian who came from a very distinguished academic background.

DB *Much like yourself.*

Yes, much like myself. My parents would get a big kick out of that. They didn't even know what the word "academic" meant. But Staughton Lynd wanted to teach at a black college. He was a very, very politically committed person. I had just hired him. It was summer. In the fall he was going to start working at Spelman College. We decided to climb a mountain together to get acquainted. My son and daughter came along. They were little kids, twelve, maybe, ten. In the course of that hike up the mountain Staughton and I talked about everything in the world: world politics, national politics, history, and so on. What was interesting to me was that here was Staughton from this very elite background, Harvard, Columbia, distinguished family, and here was I. My parents were distinguished, but not in the same way. My father was a distinguished waiter in a restaurant. My mother was a distinguished mother. We grew up in a working class environment. Here we were, two different backgrounds, and both of us seemed to agree totally on every political and social issue there was. What it reinforced for me, if I didn't know it before, is how you can't simply assume from people's background what their ideas or commitments would be, and you therefore should be open to people of whatever background to understand that the possibility exists for anyone of any background to become socially conscious.

DB *Why did you include your 1978 essay, "Upton Sinclair and Sacco & Vanzetti," in* The Reader?

I guess one, because I had also been interested in the case of Sacco and Vanzetti. It was one of those historical events that transforms the thinking of a lot of people. You can point to such things, to certain events in history which affect huge numbers of people beyond the boundaries of the event itself. The Sacco and Vanzetti case was one of those. Two Italian immigrants, anarchists, accused of murder and holdup, tried by a very prejudiced judge and jury, a totally absurd trial from the standpoint of justice, sentenced to death, an international campaign for their release lasting over years and years, but finally they are executed. The case had always interested me. And Upton Sinclair had always interested me because as a teenager he was one of the great literary influences in my life. I read not only *The Jungle*, which is the most famous work, but *Oil*, *The Brass Check*, exposés of the oil industry, of journalism, and this novel *Boston*, which was about the Sacco and Vanzetti case. I knew the novel. I had read it years ago. So when a publisher approached me to write the introduction to a reissue of *Boston*, I happily agreed to do it. For one thing, because I wanted to connect the case of Sacco and Vanzetti with problems of law and justice today and problems of capital punishment today, which are still with us, more and more with us as Republicans and Democrats together pass what they call a crime bill in which they extend the list of crimes for which people will be put to death. So this is an issue which people need to think about. That's why I wanted to include that essay.

DB *The chair of the Pulitzer Prize committee said of Sinclair's book,* Boston, *that it would have won the prize had it not been for its "socialistic tendencies." An unforgivable crime, clearly.*

It's not the first time that politics has entered into the dispensation of prizes. From time to time a mistake is made and somebody is awarded a prize. And sometimes, even more rarely, somebody is awarded a prize and they reject the prize because the prize represents an establishment which they don't want to be identified with. It just now happened. Adrienne Rich was going to be one of the national fellows in the arts. She was to be presented a prize by President Clinton. She refused, saying that she wanted in some way to protest against what this administration has done to poor people. I thought that was a courageous act.

DB *Sinclair was known also as a muckraker. It was an extraordinary period in American journalism where there were journals, magazines, newspapers devoted to uncovering corruption, both corporate as well as government.*

McClure's magazine, for instance, which had a good circulation. They published the articles of Ida Tarbell on Rockefeller and the oil monopolies. They published articles of Lincoln Steffens on corporate corruption and business-government connections. It was a time when you didn't have the kind of concentration of control in the media that you have today. You know more about that than anyone. I started to say you're one of the victims of it, but I don't think of you as a victim. You're one of the guerrilla fighters in this jungle where the helicopters of Disney and Turner are hovering over you.

DB *But this muckraking tradition came out of the Gay Nineties, a period much like the 1990s, where there was an enormous increase in wealth. The robber barons of that period were making money hand over fist.*

That's true. What also came out of that period, as you say the Gay Nineties—I like those titles, the Roaring Twenties, the Gay Nineties, the Era of Good Feeling—a period of the rise of great wealth and trusts, was the populist movement, the socialist movement at the turn of the century, the IWW. It seems to me that the muckraking that was going on was itself a response to the fact that there existed to the left of the muckrakers the Socialist Party and the IWW, Eugene Debs and Mother Jones, great labor struggles taking place creating an atmosphere of class struggle which I think at least some of the press needed to deal with.

DB *Sinclair ran for governor of California in 1934 on what he called EPIC, End Poverty In California. What did Franklin D. Roosevelt, the New Deal President, think of Sinclair's campaign?*

It's a sad story. Upton Sinclair, the socialist, actually ran in the Democratic primary first and beat out all the other Democratic primary candidates for the party's nomination. Some of his Socialist Party comrades were very offended by the fact that he would switch to the Democratic Party. But he wanted to become governor and he thought that this was the way to do it. He ran for governor on this program, EPIC. He wrote a pamphlet called "How I as Governor Ended Poverty in California," in which he explained how he would do this. He would confiscate large amounts of unused wealth and use that wealth for education and health and housing. In other words, try to follow the Socialist principle of production for use and not for profit, to each according to his needs. It was a wonderful program. I think he would have won in 1934 with that program. People were ready for it. But he was attacked on all sides. People on the left, I think very stupidly, attacked him for running under the Democratic Party. In fact, they ran candidates against him, a Progressive Party candidate, a Socialist Party candidate, which drew votes away from him and was a great boon to the Republican Party candidate. Very significantly, Franklin D. Roosevelt, whose support would have meant a lot, withdrew his support from Sinclair. He kept mum. Roosevelt, who gave his support very openly to Southern racist senators and governors in their campaigns, would not support Upton Sinclair, the socialist. He was afraid of what he would be labeled. He was very Clintonish at that moment.

DB *In 1943 Sinclair finally did win the Pulitzer Prize, but not for one of his political novels.*

At that point he began to write the Lanny Budd series, much more mainstream adventure stories, liberal in its politics but no more than that. This was much more acceptable.

DB *What do you think about using historical events like the Sacco and Vanzetti case in a novel?*

The line between what is called "fiction" and what is called "non-fiction" is not at all a very distinct one. There are ways in which a work of fiction can capture the reality of a situation more accurately than a work of non-fiction. For instance, when I was teaching 1930s history, instead of giving my students the standard historical text and the statistics on the 1930s, the unemployment, the soup lines, the facts of what legislation was passed, I had them read John Steinbeck's *The Grapes of Wrath*. It's a fictional account of what happens to a family in the 1930s in the Depression. A student, anybody, reading *The*

Grapes of Wrath is going to get the most vivid picture of what the Depression meant to human beings, something that no staid academic account can do. And in that sense it's better history than history. History which has the facts but which is shorn of the human impact of events is to my mind not valuable history.

DB   *The seventieth anniversary of Sacco and Vanzetti's execution was just marked. When Boston was reissued, you noted there was again quite a bit of controversy in Massachusetts and New York. You sort of ask rhetorically, There must be some good reason why a case, at that time fifty years old, its principals dead, generates such emotions.*

I think it's because the issue of how a just system operates is still very much with us. The factors that operate in the Sacco and Vanzetti case and that led to their execution, the factors of, Who are the defendants? Are they rich or poor? Are they Americans or foreign-born? Are they ordinary folk or radical critics of the government? Those factors, all of which combined to put Sacco and Vanzetti into the electric chair, are factors which still operate in our courtrooms today. Take the case of Mumia Abu-Jamal, who is a black man sitting on death row in Pennsylvania. Here he is, a black man, a radical. He doesn't have much money. He can't hire O.J. Simpson's lawyers. I don't want to pick on just those lawyers. You can pick on any rich person's lawyers. They're not available to somebody like Mumia Abu-Jamal. You put all those factors together and he ends up on death row. So the Sacco and Vanzetti case still resonates today because the justice system is still based on wealth, class, race.

DB   *Leonard Weinglass, who is one of Abu-Jamal's attorneys, has documented that the overwhelming majority of death row inmates, as well as those who are executed, is African-American.*

There have been lots of studies made on this and studies presented to the Supreme Court try to get the Supreme Court to say, Obviously race has played a critical factor in who gets executed in this country. Therefore we can't allow capital punishment, because it violates the equal protection of the law, the Fourteenth Amendment. The Supreme Court has never wanted to come to that conclusion. One of these days, if there is a powerful enough public campaign, they will have to do it.

DB *Make the argument against the death penalty, and make it to the grandmother whose grandchild was killed in the Oklahoma City day care center. What would you say to her?*

This is the reason why capital punishment is popular. When they take polls, they show that 75% or 80% of Americans believe in capital punishment. We must also say that the polls' percentages were not that great fifteen or twenty years ago, before they began a public campaign by politicians on the issue of capital punishment. But still, what I would say to the grandmother is, I can understand, and I think of it myself. I think that if something happened to my grandchildren, if they were in such a bombing, then my anger, my rage against whoever did this, would be the reaction of most people: This person should be put to death. That would be my first reaction. But when I think about it, I think, What good will that do? First of all, it won't bring back the dead to life. Will it change anything? Will it deter other people from doing the same thing? If we kill Timothy McVeigh, who was convicted of the bombing, will this then prevent other bombings? It never has worked that way. People who are fanatic, who bomb and kill others, do not rationally weigh the consequences of whether they'll go to prison for life or whether they'll be executed. So it's not going to have any effect on the future. And one thing that executing somebody like McVeigh or anybody in a murder case does is to take our eye away from the fundamental causes of murder in a society. We ought to look at those fundamental causes. What is it that makes people desperate? What creates the Timothy McVeighs? You can trace Timothy McVeigh's anger back to what the government did to people, to when the government itself was responsible for the killing of people in Waco, Texas. They attacked these people in this building. They threw tear gas in. Fires were set. This infuriated McVeigh and lots of other people. Of course that doesn't justify what they did. But my point is that behind the murderous acts of people you find deep grievances. What we should be doing is thinking about these grievances instead of focusing on killing the person who did this act. What we do is perpetuate the cycle of violence. The government killed the people at Waco. McVeigh kills the people in Oklahoma City. We kill McVeigh. Somebody else will kill somebody else. The cycle will go on until we break into that cycle and try to create the conditions of life in this country where people will not be unemployed, desperate, angry at the government. That's the only thing we can do.

DB   *For years death penalty advocates were making the deterrence argument. They don't make that argument any more, because the documentation refutes it. They are arguing now in Biblical terms. An eye for an eye. The punishment fits the crime. You murdered someone, you deserve to die.*

There are a number of problems with that. The eye for an eye and tooth for a tooth just continues endless violence. If the government then takes an eye, then somebody else might want to take the eye of the government. There's another problem. The way the odds are now constituted in the killing of people, governments kill far more people than private individuals do. They are not held to account. They bomb people. They kill people in war. Police kill people again and again in what is called the course of their duty, but they kill unarmed people, suspects and so on. There's no eye for an eye or tooth for a tooth that operates there. In other words, there's a lot of hypocrisy in the eye for an eye and tooth for a tooth argument because that's not the way it has worked. There are other passages in the Bible that suggest compassion and doing unto others as you would have others do unto you. There is a passage in the Bible that suggests that you should turn the other cheek, that you should *not* have an eye for an eye. You can pick whatever part of the Bible you want. But the idea of simply killing somebody in retribution is just a way of perpetuating killing in our society.

DB   *Do you know what Mahatma Gandhi said about an eye for an eye? It leaves everyone blind. The Harvard economist Richard Freeman has recently pointed out that 7% of the U.S. male work force is either in jail or is somehow engaged in the criminal justice system, on parole or probation. What does that tell you about not only law and order but about the U.S. economy?*

It tells us that there are a large number of people in the U.S. who are economically destitute and desperate. These are the people who end up in prison. That's why we have a million and a half people in prison and five or six million more just out of prison or on parole or on probation. I remember when I was going into prisons and talking to guards and prison psychiatrists and inmates, it was very, very clear that people in prison are poor people. They arrived in prison because of acts they committed that came out of the desperation of their circumstances. There's a reason why the U.S. has the biggest rate of imprisonment in the world: the extremes of wealth and poverty. So long as you have those extremes of wealth and poverty, you're going to have crimes being committed. You're going to have to build more and more jails.

DB *Let me put you in a different set of shoes right now. Let's say you were the father of someone who was convicted of a crime and was sentenced to death and executed. Twenty years later it's revealed that evidence was not brought forth during the trial, and people recanted their testimony and in fact lied. How might you feel?*

Unspeakably angry at the system, which is another point against capital punishment. You're never really sure. Sometimes you're sure. Somebody confesses, says, I did it. Sometimes the confession is forced, coerced in some way. But there have been many instances in which people have been sentenced to death or sentenced to long prison sentences and then it turned out that they had been framed by the authorities.

DB *You write, "The American system keeps control not only by a lottery of rewards (only a few make it but everyone has a chance), but also by a lottery of punishment."*

The lottery of punishment meaning, just as the lottery of rewards is skewed on behalf of the few who get the rewards, the lottery of punishment is skewed on behalf of those people at the bottom of society who can't afford lawyers and who find themselves in trouble with the law because they are unemployed and desperate. They turn to drugs or robbery or may turn to nothing, just find themselves on the streets accosted by a policeman and accused of something. It takes just the imprisonment of a relatively small number of people to create an atmosphere of fear of the authorities, a legitimate fear, by people who live in neighborhoods where they are subject to arrest any time that somebody in authority decides that they need to pull somebody in. They'll find a suspect for a crime that has been committed.

DB *Should I release you from your sentence of this interview now? Do you feel you've served enough time?*

I think I should at least be paroled.

The Future of History

July 27 and 28, 1998

DB *In* The Zinn Reader, *you write, "Important to me as I was becoming conscious of the crucial question of class was to read Karl Marx's* The Communist Manifesto.*" 1998 marks the 150th anniversary of* The Manifesto. *There have been new editions and public meetings around this event. The question arises, Is Marx relevant today? If so, how?*

I decided to deal with the question of the relevance of Marx even before this 150th anniversary, to show how far in advance I am of the general culture. I decided to do that by writing a play about him. It's called *Marx in Soho,* a one-person play, which I mentioned in a previous interview. To answer your question, the reason I wanted to do something about Marx is because I think he has important things to say.

There are some things that he said in the nineteenth century that turn out to be inadequate for an understanding of what the world is like today. Clearly, he could not anticipate so much of what has happened since then. Like a lot of people on the left, he had a foreshortened view of how long it would take for a socialist revolution to come about. There was a point where he and Engels thought the revolutions in Europe of 1848 would lead to workers' revolutions. They did not. They showed their disappointment.

So he did not really figure on capitalism's ability to survive and on the ingeniousness of the system in devising obstacles to revolution and its power in suppressing revolutionary movements and its ability to wean the working class and its consciousness away from the idea of revolutionary change. The U.S. is probably the primary illustration of that, and although Marx followed events in the U.S. in the mid-nineteenth century and was a correspondent for a while of the *New York Tribune,* he could not, and I don't know that anyone could, anticipate that the American system would be able to fend off revolutionary movements by a combination of tactics. I say "tactics" as if they were deliberate, but I think that probably it's not an accurate description to call them tactics. Let's say there are a number of developments in

American capitalism that made it possible for the system to survive. One of them was the fact that capitalism in the U.S., drawing upon the enormous wealth of this country, was able to respond to workers' movements by giving concessions, respond to unionism by agreeing to raise wages and lower hours. There were a lot of struggles to force the system to do that, but they did that. The system responded to economic crises by reforms, as it did in the 1930s under the New Deal. In doing so, responding with more and more reforms, it created a more satisfied section of the working class which then was not ripe for a workers' revolution, and which has remained content with the system or, when it became discontented, did not become discontented with capitalism as a system but became discontented with specific manifestations of the system. Most working people in the U.S. do not see the problems they have as systemic, but as problems which are correctable by reforms. So the system, by having the wealth sufficient to distribute more goodies to sections of the working class and yet maintain huge profits for itself, has been able to sustain itself.

At the time of World War I, W.E.B. Du Bois, certainly one of the most far-sighted of American intellectuals, saw that the American system was giving some rewards to its workers and was able to do this on the basis of its exploitation of people abroad. He saw the imperialism of World War I, of the Western powers, and he saw that the Western powers, by drawing out the wealth of the Middle East and Latin America and Asia, was able thereby to give some small part of its profits to its own working class and therefore enlist that working class in a kind of national unity which then enabled them to call this working class to war and sustain that war.

As I said, Marx did not foresee this very sophisticated ability of capitalism to create a certain degree of satisfaction among just enough of the working class, certainly not all of the working class, but just enough to give it a buffer against revolution. There's a big difference between having a working class which is eighty percent of the population and is seething with anger at the system and a working class of which half has been given enough goodies to be content, leaving a minority in desperate poverty. The minority may be an important one, in the U.S. it may be forty million people who are in desperate circumstances without health care, with a high incidence of child mortality, but still not enough to make the kind of workers' revolution that Marx and Engels were hoping for.

So Marx didn't see that kind of development. I think he also did not see, and this was pointed out by Paul Sweezy and Paul Baran when they wrote their post-World War II, post-Marxist analysis of capitalism that the economic crisis that Marxists expected to happen after the end of World War II did not take place because of the militarization of capitalism. A kind of military Keynesianism was in operation, where by spending a huge amount of money on military contracts, the government was creating employment and was giving shots of "drugs," in the long run poisonous but in the short run sustaining the system. Baran and Sweezy saw this militarization as one of the ways in which capitalism was able to survive. And Marx did not really foresee that.

On the other hand, there were analyses that Marx made of the capitalist system which turn out to be very, very true, and very perceptive. Probably the most obvious one is the increasing concentration and centralization of capital on a worldwide scale. What we talk about now as the global economy, as globalization, Marx had foreseen. He saw the world becoming more and more interconnected economically. He saw the corporations turning into megacorporations and the mergers and the possession of the material resources of the world becoming concentrated in fewer and fewer hands. Very often it's said Marx talked about the immiseration of the proletariat and the concomitant increasing wealth of the upper classes, the polarization of wealth and poverty. And very often it's said that Marx was wrong about this. We haven't had this. In the U.S. it doesn't look that clear because of this large middle class which is not at one pole or the other. But if you look at it on a worldwide scale, world capitalism has moved exactly in that direction. If you take the wealth of the rich countries as against the wealth of the poor countries, and especially if you take the wealth of the upper income brackets in the rich countries against the ninety percent of the people in the poor countries, you have a polarization of wealth which is more stark than it was in the nineteenth century.

DB *So in terms of looking at and understanding political economy, there is much that is relevant in Marx's analyses.*

I think his analysis of capitalism remains very relevant, and his perception that the profit motive was ruinous for the human race remains, I think, a great insight. We see that the drive of corporations for profit is done at the expense of human beings all over the world.

One of the things Marx pointed out was that once money was introduced into the world economy, the pursuit of wealth became infinite. It was no longer a matter of material possessions, of land, as it was in feudal times, now there was no longer a limit to the accumulation of wealth once money was introduced. This endless pursuit of money has led to all sorts of dangerous and evil developments, because the pursuit of money has led chemical companies to pollute the air and water, has led arms manufacturers to create monstrous weapons of destruction without regard to how they will be used or against whom they will be used. His analysis of the evils of profit as a motive for production I think is more true now than it every was.

DB *Those who trumpet the virtues of capitalism point out that the USSR appropriated Marx and his name and the good name of socialism. Since the Soviet Union collapsed in disarray both Marx's analyses and a socialist political philosophy are therefore discredited.*

That's what's being said. Marxism would only be discredited if indeed the Soviet Union had created the kind of society that Marx and Engels foresaw as a socialist society, and then collapsed. But when Marx and Engels talked about the dictatorship of the proletariat, they had a very special conception of what that meant. It meant that the majority of the people, the working class, would be in charge of the society. They did not mean by dictatorship of the proletariat that a political party would represent itself as total spokesperson for the working class. In fact, not only would a political party not be the spokesman, but certainly not a central committee, certainly not a Politburo, certainly not one person. That kind of dictatorship was not envisioned by Marx and Engels when they talked about the dictatorship of the proletariat.

In fact, at one point, Marx was talking about the Paris Commune of 1871 and the remarkably democratic character of the Paris Commune, the *communards*, the people who gathered and legislated, made decisions in the context of endless daily, hourly, twenty-four-hours-a-day discussions in the streets of Paris by the people of Paris. Marx talked about those remarkable several months when democracy flourished in Paris, the Paris Commune. He said, You want to know what I mean by the dictatorship of the proletariat? Look at the Paris Commune. The Soviet Union certainly did not follow that. And when Marx talked about what a socialist society would look like, he certainly did not expect that a socialist society would set up gulags, would imprison dissidents and shoot not just capitalists, but fellow revolutionaries, as was done in both the Soviet Union and in China. So the police state and the totalitarian nature of the Soviet Union were very foreign to Marx and Engels. They saw the dictatorship of the proletariat as a temporary phenomenon during which the socialist character of society would become more and more communal, more and more democratic, and that the state, as they said, would become less and less necessary. Marx and Engels talked in *The Communist Manifesto* about their aim being the free development of the individual.

The Soviet Union and other countries that have called themselves Marxist and have established police states acted in a way very, very contrary, I believe, to the spirit of Marx's ideas. So that when the Soviet Union collapsed in the late 1980s, and it happened with other countries in Eastern Europe, I personally did not feel this as a sign that socialism was therefore discredited. To me it was always a bastard form of socialism, one that couldn't even be called socialism. Actually, I was very glad that with the disintegration of the Soviet Union you could no longer associate the Soviet Union and socialism, you could no longer say, This is a place where socialism exists. To me it seemed that now the air could be cleared and that we could begin to think of socialism for instance as it was thought of in the early part of the century in the U.S., before the Soviet Union existed, when the Socialist Party in the U.S. was a powerful force, when its candidate for President got close to a million votes. You had socialist newspapers all over the country read probably by several million people. At that time the I.W.W., the Industrial Workers of the World, was a very powerful force in organizing strikes and struggles around the country.

To me it is very interesting that socialism in this country was at its most influential before a Soviet Union existed. Because then the people could, without the imposition of some foreign, distorted example, take a look at the ideas of socialism. It made a lot of sense to them. They could see Eugene Debs and Mother Jones and Emma Goldman and Jack London and Lincoln Steffens and see obviously admirable people in the U.S. who had turned to socialism because they saw what capitalism was doing to people. Socialism at that time represented a simple common-sense idea, that you take the wealth of the country and try to use it in a rational and humane way.

DB *The Reaganites take credit for the collapse of the Soviet Union. They say Reagan's aggressive weapons policy, expansion of the military helped to bankrupt the USSR. What's your take on that? Do you have an alternative view on why the Soviet Union collapsed?*

I always have an alternative view. It's not just that I don't want to give Reagan credit for anything, although of course I don't want to give Reagan credit for anything. I have no doubt that the militarization of the Soviet economy was a factor in impoverishing the Soviet Union in terms of being able to do things for its people. No doubt about that. But that was a very long-term development. It didn't happen only under Reagan. It's a long-term development ever since World War II. The Soviet Union and the U.S. engaging in an arms race and both countries spending an exorbitant amount of their national wealth on the military. As a result, leaving the society impoverished, unable to use its wealth for human needs. So I don't doubt that was a factor. It also has been a factor in the U.S. in causing the U.S. to have a social service structure which is less generous to its people than, let's say, the social service sector of much poorer countries, like the countries of Scandinavia or New Zealand or France and Germany with their universal health care systems. So I don't doubt that that was a factor in causing more and more discontent in the Soviet Union.

Without pretending to know exactly and certainly what caused the Soviet Union to collapse, it seems to me that one of the truly important factors was the gradual growing discontent with the system, with the police state, with the lack of freedom. I'm thinking of the growing ties of the Soviet Union with the rest of the world, you might say the phenomenon that Marx described, that the world would become more interconnected, that people and goods would travel more and more across borders, culture would be disseminated all over the world, people would get to know about what's happening in other countries. For people in the Soviet Union, as more travel took place, as radio and television brought information to them, I think their own society became more and more distasteful to them. Restrictions on their travel, on their freedom of speech became more and more onerous. I think they developed a kind of underground of dissent. We know that there was an underground press, underground literature, *samizdat*, self-publication, literally, of things that circulated unofficially and spread subversive ideas. All of these had a kind of corrosive effect on a society that was very tyrannical. I guess I believe that tyrannies ultimately, sometimes it takes ten years and sometimes it takes forty or sixty years, must collapse. Whoever happens to be the leader of a rival country at the time the collapse takes place will take credit for it, as Reagan did in this case.

DB *To what extent did Western European, U.S. and even Japanese hostility to the nascent Soviet state, economic sanctions, embargoes, in fact outright invasions, contribute to developing a hard line and totalitarianism within the regime itself?*

It's a tough question to answer. There were the immediate attempts to destroy the Bolshevik Revolution right then and there; 1918–1919, you have the expeditionary forces sent by Western powers, including the U.S. under Woodrow Wilson, to the Soviet Union to try to crush the new revolutionary government, and the continued hostility of the West to the Soviet Union. I have no doubt that that contributed to the hardness of the Soviet state. But I also am very reluctant to justify the development of the police state on the grounds that they had to do this in order to fend off their enemies. I think that's too easy an explanation and a justification for what to me is inexcusable. Although there is some truth to it, it became an excuse and a rationale for maintenance of tight control over the state by a small number of people and finally by one person. So I don't really accept that as justification for what happened. In fact, I would argue that the security of the Soviet Union would have been enhanced by an atmosphere of freedom, that there would have been a solidarity among the Soviet population in defense of a state which was both socialist in its economic egalitarianism and democratic in its political structure. There would have been a loyalty to such a state which would have made the Soviet Union much stronger in relation to its potential enemies. Almost certainly it would have prevented the kind of collapse that just took place.

DB *One of the interesting figures of that era is Leon Trotsky. He was an early critic of Lenin. He later joined Lenin and became the leader of the Red Army. Then he was trumped by Stalin in a power play. Some people have looked back at that wistfully and perhaps romantically, saying, Had*

Trotsky emerged, it's one of those what-if questions of history, the path and development of the Soviet Union as it proceeded under Stalin would have been remarkably different.

As you suggested, it's so hard to know what would have happened if Trotsky had taken leadership of the Soviet Union instead of Stalin. I suppose it's fair to say that history wouldn't have developed in exactly the same way. But would it have developed in a totally different way, would the Soviet Union have become both socialist and democratic? Looking at Trotsky's record, I kind of doubt it. I am looking at the fact that Trotsky was in charge of the Red Army at the time that the Red Army destroyed the rebellion at Kronstadt right after the Bolshevik Revolution. This is something that I think needs to be considered very carefully by anybody who thinks that Trotsky was humanitarian and would have set the Soviet Union on a different path. The Kronstadt rebels—Kronstadt is a naval base outside of Leningrad—were dissatisfied with the conditions of their work and their lives. They had looked to the Bolshevik Revolution as a solution to their problems, but they found that the leaders of the Revolution were indifferent to their demands and their needs, and they rebelled. They were crushed by the Red Army under Trotsky and Lenin. To me that's a sign of the fact that the new Soviet Union was not going to tolerate dissent. Maxim Gorky pointed this out. There was a brief period after the Revolution when it was possible to publish newspapers that were somewhat critical. Gorky, of course, had a great literary reputation and could say things that other people could not say. So he published a little newspaper shortly after the Revolution called *Novaya Vremya* (New Times). In it he expressed his horror at the fact that the Soviet government was sending the police to break up demonstrations of protesters who were asking for reforms. I trust Gorky, I guess. I trust his sensibility. Emma Goldman and Alexander Berkman, who were deported to the Soviet Union from the U.S. after World War I, personally escorted to the boat by J. Edgar Hoover, arrived in the Soviet Union prepared to welcome the Bolshevik Revolution, even though they were anarchists and suspicious of centralized government. They thought, Maybe this will be a step on the way to democratic society. But what they saw immediately was Lenin and Trotsky and the government putting anarchists and other dissidents in prison, suppressing their newspapers.

So I'm dubious about Trotsky, although he may have been different than Stalin. Maybe he would have killed half as many people, I don't know what he would have done. But his record does not suggest that he would have created a more humane socialism.

DB *Among American sympathizers with the new Soviet state in the 1920s and 1930s, does your reading of that period indicate that there may have been rather distorted views of what was actually going on in the Soviet Union?*

By American sympathizers, I suppose you mean mainly the Communist Party in the U.S. The Communist Party was created after World War I. The Socialist Party had been destroyed by its leaders being put in jail, not only its leaders, but almost a thousand people put in jail during World War I for opposing the war. So there was a kind of vacuum at the end of World War I and then the Communist Party arose in 1919 and developed slowly in the 1920s and became a more powerful organization in the 1930s with the onset of the Depression. The Communist Party looked upon the Soviet Union as representing the fulfillment of the socialist dream. There have been a number of studies of the history of the Communist Party. Analyses fall into two camps. One of them says very simply: The Communist Party slavishly followed the Soviet Union and was subservient to Soviet objectives and therefore the Party line twisted and turned according to whatever Soviet policy was. Indeed, you can see this most clearly in the events around World War II, where the Soviet Union had signed a nonaggression pact with Hitler on the eve of World War II. The Communist Party accepted that on the grounds that this was a tactic to deflect the West, which had been anti-Soviet, and to save the Soviet Union. When the war began between Hitler and France and England, and the Soviet Union still had its nonaggression pact with Hitler, the line of the Communist Party of the U.S. was, Stay out of the war. It's an imperialist war. The Yanks are not coming. That was the slogan.

Then, when the Soviet Union was invaded on June 22, 1941, immediately the line changed. Now it's no longer an imperialist war. Now it's a people's war. Now the Soviet Union is involved. So yes, the policies of the Communist Party shifted according to Soviet needs. This perception by one group of analysts of the American Communist

Party has led them to say, It's very simple. The Communist Party was a tool of the Soviet Union.

There's another view: while it is true the top leadership of the Communist Party followed the Soviet line and adjusted its policy accordingly, the rank and file Communists in the U.S. did not join the party because of the existence of the Soviet Union. They did see the Soviet Union as an ideal. The information that was given to them about the Soviet Union was that it was doing wonderful things for its people: full employment and social security and the elimination of race prejudice. They were given a false picture of the Soviet Union, and they believed that. But that wasn't the main reason for rank and file Communists joining the Communist Party. The main reason was the conditions here in the U.S., the Depression. Communists were in the lead in organizing unemployment councils, organizing tenants, organizing the labor movement, organizing the CIO, speaking out against racism. When some young black men in Alabama faced the death penalty for some trumped-up rape charges against them—the Scottsboro Boys—the Communist Party sprang to their defense. So the Communist Party had a record in this country of standing for progressive and decent causes. That, according to this second view of the party, was primary for most rank and file Communists. Proof of the fact that this was primary is that when more and more information came out about the Soviet Union, as in 1956 when Khrushchev delivered his address to the 20th Party Congress and for the first time sensationally exposed the crimes of Stalin before the world, there was a great exodus from the Communist Party. When the Soviet Union invaded Hungary there was another exodus from the party. In other words, when the people who had joined the party because it was antifascist and pro-labor and egalitarian learned the facts about the Soviet Union, they left the party in droves. The second view of the party is closer to my view.

DB *Were you struck at all by the nonviolent transformation of the Soviet Union and its neighboring satellite states, with the exception of Rumania? Here were virtual military dictatorships undergoing a peaceful transfer of government.*

I think that's a very fascinating development and a very important piece of history for us to look at. What it does is reinforce the notion that it is possible to bring about important social change without violence, without a bloodbath. To me, it is a vindication of the notion that we should give up the idea of using military force to bring about social change. In fact, social change can come about by the actions of a great social movement. The resort to military force to bring about social change, the resort to armed insurrection or what the revolutionary movement might call armed struggle is evidence that the revolutionary movement has not built up enough support among the population. Once it builds up that mass support, if it can create among the masses of the people resistance to the ongoing government tyranny, that tyranny will not be able to stand for long. It will not be able to move. Its armed forces will not go along. Its service sectors will not serve. I think that's what happened in these countries. As soon as you have mass outpourings of people into the streets, and this happened in East Germany, too, and they could see that the resistance was overwhelming, they could not function any more. So to me this is very powerful evidence. Despite the argument that it is necessary to make war in order to overthrow tyranny, the developments in Eastern Europe reinforced the notion that war is not the way to do it. Or take the Soviet Union as an example. We came very close in the U.S. to the decision to use nuclear weapons against the Soviet Union in order to destroy it. The tyranny fell by itself, mostly from internal causes.

Eastern Europe is not the only example of this. Spain, I think, is another interesting one. The Franco dictatorship lasted a long time. It seemed to a lot of observers, and certainly to people who had fought in Spain, members of the Abraham Lincoln Brigade, that Franco would not be overthrown without another bloody civil war. That civil war in Spain had cost a million lives from 1936-1939. When Franco dies years later and the regime collapses, you don't get an ideal state. You don't get a socialist state. You don't get democratic socialism. You certainly get a more liberal state. They've done away with fascism in Spain. You create openings for change to take place without a bloody civil war.

I think one of the most striking examples of the idea that important social change can take place and should take place without massive violence is what happened in South Africa, where people thought that you could not get rid of apartheid without a bloody civil war. To me it was interesting that the African National Congress, which certainly was not a timid organization and was ready to engage in sabotage and even individual acts of violence, was not willing to have an all-out civil war in South Africa. They knew that it would result in millions of people being killed, most of them black South Africans. They were willing to spend more time, more energy, utilize a variety of tactics and ultimately apartheid collapsed in South Africa. Who would have predicted that Mandela, imprisoned on Robbens Island for twenty-seven years, would become leader of the new South Africa? And while the new South Africa has not solved fundamental problems, no question about that, still, apartheid as it existed no longer exists. Black political power at least creates the possibility of a change that was not possible under the old regime. It took place on the basis of a complexity of tactics that did not include armed rebellion.

DB *You also wrote a play about Emma Goldman, entitled* Emma. *It's been performed in the U.S., Japan and England. What drew you to her?*

I knew nothing about Emma Goldman. I knew nothing about most things. Then at a certain point in our lives we learn something, and then we claim we knew those things from birth. I vaguely had heard of Emma Goldman from reading a book when I was a teenager called *Critics and Crusaders*, which is long out of print but had a very important influence on me. It was a book of essays on different radicals in American history. There was a chapter on each one, including Emma Goldman, the anarchist and feminist. I had read that chapter on her, but had pretty much forgotten about it, as she was forgotten by American culture for a long time. She had been a very powerful figure at the turn of the century. She was shoved into the background not just by the general culture, but by left culture, because the Communist Party was the dominant force in the U.S. in the 1930s and 1940s. Emma Goldman was anti-Communist. She had written a book, a very strong attack on the Soviet Union, as a result of her experiences. She was relegated to obscurity not just by the establishment, but by the left.

I did not know anything about her until I encountered at some meeting in Pennsylvania in the mid or late 1960s a fellow historian named Richard Drinnon who told me he had written a biography of her called *Rebel in Paradise*. You know how it is, when you meet somebody who has written a book you very often want to go and read that book. I read it. It's a wonderful book, beautifully written. Drinnon is among American historians one of the most eloquent of writers. His biography of Emma Goldman is stunning. It led me to read her autobiography, *Living My Life*, which I recommend all the time and which I have my students read. What fascinated me was that here we were in the 1960s, the New Left had distanced itself from traditional Communist Party doctrine and, without calling itself anarchist, had many of the sensibilities of the anarchist in being anti-state, anti-dogmatism and wanting to make revolutionary changes in the culture simultaneously with changes in the politics and economics. So Emma Goldman fitted, in my view, a new left conception of the universe.

I found that my students, far from seeing her as an antiquated and irrelevant figure, as I feared at one time when I began to give them her writings, were excited by her ideas and her approach to life, her powerful feminism, her anarchism, her position against the state, against capitalism, against religion, against all of the traditional rules of sexual behavior, of marriage. She was a free spirit. It fitted the free-spirited culture of the 1960s. The play was a matter of the desire and the opportunity joining. When the Vietnam War was going on, I was, as so many people were, totally preoccupied with the war. In the late 1960s and early 1970s, the things that I wrote, my teaching, the talks I was giving around the country, and the teach-ins were all in one way or another connected with the Vietnam War. When the war ended in 1975, I was relieved of a lot of work. I finally saw an opening to do something I had wanted to do for some time, to write a play. The subject became Emma Goldman and that little group of anarchists with which she was associated at the turn of the century.

DB *What informed and influenced your play writing? Did you have any models, were you interested in Bertolt Brecht's work, for example?*

I was interested in Brecht's work. There were a number of influences in my life that led me toward play writing. First there were people in my own family who had been involved in the theater. My wife was an actress for a while in Atlanta and here in Cambridge. My daughter was in the Altanta production of the *Diary of Anne Frank* in 1962. She played Anne Frank and won a prize as the best actress of the year in Atlanta. Our son was a musician and an actor and devoted his life to the theater, which he is still doing, running a little theater

in Wellfleet on Cape Cod. So my whole family was involved in theater except me. But I was interested in theater. My wife and I, when
we lived in New York, although we didn't have much money, went to
see plays by Arthur Miller. We saw the first Broadway productions of
Death of a Salesman and Tennessee Williams' *Streetcar Named Desire*.
We saw Marlon Brando and Jessica Tandy, sitting in the cheapest
seats possible, way up, but loving the theater.

So when the war ended I had an opportunity and more free time,
and I decided I would write a play. Emma Goldman and anarchism
became my theme. My son, who was at that time acting in New York,
was the first director of the first production of the play in New York.

DB *Can you give a little more detail on Brecht? He's seen as the
quintessential political dramatist.*

Brecht certainly was one of the influences in my development as
a playwright, if I can assume that I developed as a playwright. Brecht is
important to me. I saw a number of his plays. My wife Roslyn acted in
the *Caucasian Chalk Circle*, which was done when the Loeb Theater in
Cambridge first opened. She had a few small parts in it, along with
Jane Alexander, who also had a few small parts in it. Jane Alexander
went on to become a professional actress. My wife went on to become
ultimately a painter and artist. We saw here in Cambridge a production of *A Man's a Man*, a powerful antiwar play by Brecht, and *The
Good Woman of Setzuan* and a number of other plays. Brecht was a
brilliant playwright. Then there was *Threepenny Opera*. Brecht's politics spoke to me and his theatrical imagination spoke to me. I don't
think I've ever developed that much imagination, but then, how many
people have? I content myself with that thought. So yes, you might say
I became hooked on the theater.

When I got involved, I had a number of very happy learning
experiences. When you become a theater person, it's very different
from being an academic. You immediately become part of a group project. The academy, the university, is very isolating. Presumably you're
a member of a department and presumably you have colleagues, but it
never works that way. You really are alone. You're writing your things
alone. It's not a collective enterprise. In the theater it immediately,
inevitably becomes a collective enterprise as soon as your play is taken
over by the director. The director becomes equal, in fact more than

equal, to you. As soon as the actors come in, the set designer and cos-tumer and stage manager come into the picture, you have a little col-lective working on this project. Everybody is as eager to do this well as you are. So it was very heartwarming for me to suddenly find myself with a group of people who were all working together on this project. I had the special reward of working with my son. I couldn't say I was a traditional father who went fishing with his son, because my son was doing his music. He went with his group of rock musicians and I was doing my thing. He had left the house and was acting in New York. Suddenly here I was working together with him on this play. I remem-ber people warning me, when I told them my son was going to direct the play, saying, That's not a good idea. Directors and writers are always at odds with one another. But it turned out to be a marvelous experience. We worked together beautifully. I must admit, he was the boss. It was a revelation to me. Here I was, working as an underling to my son. He said, Look, I need you to cut this out. I need you to write a few more lines here. But it was wonderful working with him, partici-pating with him in the casting of the play.

Also, I learned a lot about the economics of the theater and about its desperate situation in a society based on profits. Sorry to get back to Marx and capitalism and the profit motive, but it pervades our entire culture. The commerce and the money element dictate what happens in the theater. It dictates that superficial plays will run on Broadway with huge budgets and be shown to huge numbers of people, and serious, important plays, because they are not going to be prof-itable, are not going to be funded. They're performed in small theaters and have short runs or they're never produced at all. Many of us have the experience that some of the best theater we've seen has been in small spaces by impecunious theater groups that don't have any money, where the actors do not get paid. To me people who work in the theater below the level of stars on Broadway are the most heroic people in our culture, along with poets and painters and writers and broadcasters of alternative radio, who struggle and struggle without much money to do something important in a culture. Actors and actresses rehearse for six weeks and go on stage every night for another six weeks and give their all, give their time, their heart, for nothing or for very little because they're in love with and believe in what they're doing. I have enormous admiration for these people.

DB *Returning to Brecht briefly, he always used to say that he was one step ahead of the Wehrmacht. He escaped from Germany and went to another country, the German army invaded. He finally ends up in the U.S. and is subjected to the political persecution that was going on here. He gave a remarkable, and I'll have to say it, theatrical performance at the House Un-American Activities Committee in, I believe, 1948.*

It was very funny. Brecht's testimony before the House Un-American Activities Committee was a time when they were investigating Hollywood. People who want to read the full transcript of it can get Eric Bentley's book *Thirty Years of Treason*, which reproduces the transcripts of actors and actresses and writers and directors who appeared before the HUAC in 1947 and 1948. Here's Bertolt Brecht, who's command of English was not huge, but it was a lot better than the HUAC's grasp of German. His testimony before them was a classic bit of theater in itself. He baffled them. They didn't know what to do with him. The answers he gave were like conundrums which led them into labyrinths of confusion out of which they never came. They would say, Mr. Brecht, is it true that you wrote the following lines in your play *The Good Woman of Setzuan*? And he would say, No, I think you don't have it quite right. Did you read that in the German? You could see the nervous tremors that developed in the members of the committee sitting there. Somebody who watched or listened to that testimony before the HUAC said it was like a zoologist being cross-examined by apes. They would not allow Brecht to make the statement that he had prepared to be delivered to the committee, a perfect example of the belief of this committee in free speech. His statement was later released and exists in printed form. It was a remarkable statement in which he ends up saying, You're worried about communism and so on, but the world that we're living in now is a world full of deep problems. In a world like this, we must be open to all sorts of ideas. We must examine all sorts of approaches. Here was Brecht lecturing these purported defenders of democracy against totalitarianism, on what freedom and democracy really are.

DB *But he was no fool, as you suggest. He had a ticket in his pocket, and he left the U.S. the next day.*

Brecht was very good at making quick escapes. He was not going to be a martyr. There are people who believe in being martyrs. Brecht had a very realistic view of the ruthlessness of the people whom he faced. He was not going to allow himself to be their victim. He immediately left.

DB *One of the great cultural figures of the twentieth century is Charlie Chaplin. He, too, was investigated by the witch hunters in Washington. Was that politically driven? Wasn't Chaplin deported?*

He was not an American citizen, and they would not allow him to stay in this country. There's no question but that it was politically driven on the basis of the fact that he'd been a supporter of various progressive and left-wing causes and because of films that he made. Although they did not want to declare his films subversive, there's no question they were. *Modern Times* was a devastating critique of the capitalist industrial system. Of course they would not want to admit that his film *The Great Dictator* was a powerful anti-fascist film at a time when so many leaders of this government were so soft on fascism. His other comedies, his silent comedies, were permeated with class consciousness, with subtle and not-so-subtle critiques of police and a system which reduced people to poverty, the tramp, the immigrant. None of that would endear him to defenders of the American establishment.

DB *Chaplin's works were not simply dry polemics. They were enormously entertaining. They were funny.*

That's what makes him even more dangerous. The system can handle dogmatic, dry and boring critics of the system. But it's absolutely infuriating to them to see somebody who is a critic, who is on the left and whose films are being watched by hundreds of millions of people around the globe, who's funny, who's entertaining. In fact, there were times when the HUAC deliberately did not call certain people to the stand because these people were too popular. I have a friend, Cheyney Ryan. He was a student activist here in Boston. That's where I got to know him. Now for years he's been teaching philosophy at the University of Oregon. He's the son of Robert Ryan, the actor. He told me, and I don't think he'd mind me repeating this. If you do, Cheyney, forgive me. His father, who was a progressive person on the left who supported anti-fascist causes and who had a real consciousness about the American system, was not called before the

HUAC, as so many other people were, because he was a popular figure in the movies. He was a kind of John Wayne figure, a hero, a tough guy, one hundred percent American. Too many Americans identified with Robert Ryan in that heroic way. He was white Anglo-Saxon, handsome, heroic, didn't fit the stereotype of the subversive. You might say they preferred to call short Jewish writers to the stand to exemplify communism, which would make it easier for bigotry to become a factor in anti-communism.

DB *What do you think the U.S. government's role should be in the arts? For example, the U.S. gives $98 million a year to the National Endowment for the Arts. It's fiercely debated. The budget comes under enormous scrutiny and discussion. What would be an ideal situation in terms of funding? Are you a purist one way or another?*

$98 million for the arts. There are countries in Western Europe where the government gives one hundred times as much money, proportionately, as the U.S. does. Denmark, Holland, Germany, England, the Scandinavian countries subsidize the arts in a far more important way than the U.S. does. Yet this pitiful amount of money, less than the amount allocated for military bands, becomes the subject of debate on whether art should be subsidized when that art sometimes is outrageous, maybe politically or culturally, because it maybe involves nudity or lesbianism or in some way is offensive to those people who are still living in another century. By another century I don't mean the twenty-first century. I mean the fourteenth. In a decent society art would be subsidized because artists need to be paid, because writers and painters need to survive. But we live in a capitalist society driven by profit and where the profit system will make the decision that artists and poets and playwrights and actors cannot make a living. When the market determines that, then a reasonable, liberal, capitalist government will make up for the inadequacy of the so-called free market and subsidize artists the way that capitalist governments in Western Europe do. It's not socialism. It's a kind of humanitarian moment for capitalism when it does that.

I remember once on a flight from Capetown, South Africa to London, I met a German woman who got on in Frankfurt. It turned out she was an actress. What are you doing in London? I'm going on vacation. She told me that she gets a salary from the German government. They don't ask her what she's going to play in, if she's going to be acting every week of the year. When there are plays, she acts in them. When there are no plays, she goes on vacation. But she is paid an annual salary, just as congressmen in this country are paid an annual salary, even though they spend a lot of time doing other things besides being in Congress. I see my son and other people in the theater struggling, devoting their life to the theater and struggling to survive economically because this so-called market system in all its beauties will not enable them to survive.

DB *When I was asking you about purity, there is one school that argues that if you accept government funding, you accept government restrictions, controls and constraints. What side do you come on in that?*

I'm not that kind of a purist, although there are many areas in which I'm a total purist, like insisting on the sophisticated audio equipment that you have when you record me. If the system impoverishes artists, and if we all are paying taxes to the government, with a good part of these taxes going for stupid things, like nuclear weapons, I think we have a right to demand that part of our taxes be used for the arts. Sure, when this happens there will be forces in the society which will then try to determine the content of these arts, but that's another fight that must be waged. So we have a double battle in the culture, one to get the government to subsidize the arts, and the second to make sure that the subsidization is not accompanied by political strings.

DB *The founding document for public broadcasting in the U.S., the Carnegie Commission Report, sought to have a mechanism to remove funding for public radio and TV from the appropriations loop. When the Public Broadcasting Act was pushed through by LBJ, it was the last of his Great Society pieces of legislation that was enacted, that mechanism was not included. There was no heat shield. Now, three decades later, we have a situation where public radio and TV are subjected to political attack by Congress, which controls the purse strings.*

It's interesting. It would be a wonderful thing to strive for to have the money that's given to the arts not subject to that kind of political pressure. The money that's given to the military is not subject to that kind of scrutiny. They don't have hearings where citizens can get up and say, I don't think our money should go for this weapon or that weapon because it's immoral. I would assume that a weapon can be more immoral than a work of art. So we have a lot of work to do in order to remove the arts from that political process, even while insisting that the arts be subsidized by public taxation.

DB *Ben Bagdikian, a veteran journalist and author of* The Media Monopoly, *perhaps taking his cue from the British system, suggests having, say, a one-dollar tax on every radio and TV that's sold. And that money would go into a fund to support public radio and TV.*

I suppose any device that would increase the amount of money available for public radio and TV would be good, but I wonder if there might be a better, more equitable way to raise that money than to tax the consumer. Sure, it's probably better than not having any money at all, but it seems to me we should tax the big broadcasters, the advertisers, put a tax on every piece of advertising that goes on TV, tax the biggies instead of the consumer. You'd raise a lot more money that way, too. That would be preferable. Of course, I have great respect for Ben Bagdikian. While I think his suggestion is preferable to what we have now, I think something that would involve a more progressive tax would be better.

DB *Boston is home to a major NPR radio station, Boston University's very own WBUR. Do you listen to NPR? What do you think of it?*

I do occasionally listen to NPR, but I'm not a regular listener. I haven't listened to it the way that a student of NPR would listen, so I can't claim to give you the fine details. NPR has the potential of doing what journalism is supposed to do, being the watchdog for society and being a sharp social critic and being absolutely unabashed in its examination of what is happening in this country in domestic and foreign policy. NPR has not fulfilled that possibility. It's hesitant and cautious. It gives us a lot of stuff on the air which is intended to be human interest stuff which I find very bland. There's a difference, for instance, in listening to WBUR and listening to Pacifica. KGNU in Boulder, alternative radio stations around the country, community radio stations, do a much better job in doing what journalism is supposed to do. During the Gulf War in 1991, I found that about the only place on radio that you could get an honest examination, a critical examination of what we were doing in the Gulf was on the alternative radio stations. NPR was playing it safe.

DB *It has two major news programs,* Morning Edition *and* All Things Considered. *Have you ever appeared on either one?*

No. I appeared once on that show that happens from 2 to 4 every day, *Talk of the Nation*, as part of a panel of three or four historians. I had a little bit of time. But NPR has never given me, I say this in a complaining voice, of course, the time and opportunity that, let's say, WBAI in New York or KPFA on the West Coast have. I've had lengthy one-hour interviews with commercial radio stations that gave me more time than NPR has given me.

DB *What would be a rational explanation for that? Not to overflatter you, but you're not an insignificant figure. Your books sell in the hundreds of thousands. You publish widely. You're fairly well known. Your lectures are well attended all over the country. Why aren't NPR's premier flagship news programs talking to you once in a while?*

Timidity, caution.

DB *They don't have your phone number.*

I'm a very hard person to reach, as you know. The same thing could be said about Noam Chomsky, even more glaringly true because Noam Chomsky, although I don't like to admit it, is better known than I am and has more to say than I do and knows more than I do on more subjects and is an international figure of merit. They don't rush to ask his opinion. I don't know if he ever has appeared on NPR, but I've never heard him on NPR.

DB *He's been on three times in about twenty-seven years. If you tune in every nine years you might hear Chomsky. Is that enough?*

Once in nine years is adequate. I'm going to tell Noam that and tell him he should be grateful that if people tune in on their radio and keep it going for nine years that ultimately they'll hear them. I think it's caution and timidity. Oh, my God, what will he say? You see the same thing on public television, if you don't mind me talking about television as well as radio. I know you keep very close control over what I say. What I do very often tune in on—I guess it's masochism—is *The NewsHour with Jim Lehrer*. As I say, it's a bit of masochism, because inevitably I'm infuriated by the limits of the discussion, certainly the limitation on who they put on the air. I'm not simply talking about their failure to put me on the air, but the fact that almost all the time their panels run from the right to the center. Maybe two degrees to the left and thirty-eight degrees to the right. Aside from the fact that they therefore do not get a real spectrum of opinion, the result is boring. A friend of mine is a stand-up comic. Some of my friends are unwittingly stand-up comics, and others are deliberately stand-up comics. This one is a deliberate stand-up comic. He does a parody of that program in which he has a panel consisting of people saying, I agree, I agree, I agree. These people are not far from one another in opinions. So there are lots of very interesting people who would lend not just a different political viewpoint but color and life to those discussions. I think of Barbara Ehrenreich, Eqbal Ahmad, Jim Hightower, Noam Chomsky, Ed Herman, and Elaine Bernard. There are all these people who would have something very vital to say and who are ignored by public radio and television.

DB *Perhaps evidence of what you are suggesting in terms of the very narrow range of debate, particularly on* The NewsHour with Jim Lehrer, *occurred in early 1998 in building up to what seemed was going to be a major U.S. attack on Iraq. One evening I tuned in and there were four present and retired military experts on. The questions ranged from, Should we invade Baghdad and seize Saddam Hussein? Should there be a lightning military special forces drop? No, we can't do that, there may be too many casualties. Should it be limited to bombing? This was all pervaded with the pronoun "we." The commentator kept asking, What should "we" do? I felt a lot better because I was involved in these important decisions. Jeff Cohen, of* Fairness and Accuracy in Reporting *calls this the "we we syndrome."*

I've noticed that many times. Television commentators, like Dan Rather in the Gulf War in 1991, talking about "we" dropped bombs yesterday on Baghdad. It's a very common thing for journalists to identify themselves with the government of the U.S., which is exactly what journalists are not supposed to do. They're supposed to be critics of the government. What you described in relation to the possible onset of the bombing of Baghdad in 1998, I found again and again. The debate takes place within very limited bounds. The questioner is not asked, Should we bomb Iraq? The question is, How shall we bomb Iraq? Or, Shall we bomb and invade or just bomb and not invade? It's especially disheartening when you think that we are all brought up to believe that we live in the exemplary democratic country in the world, a country which is so different from totalitarian states where dissident views are not allowed. Here in the U.S. we have pluralism of views, a free marketplace of ideas. Of course that pluralism is confined to a very narrow spectrum, and people are not allowed to wheel pushcarts into the marketplace.

DB *Returning again to the issue of federal funding, about $300 million goes to public radio and public TV stations in the U.S. Some people would argue, even some on the left, that it's that kind of funding that inhibits the possibility of wider debate and it should be jettisoned altogether. These stations should be completely independent and free from any kind of federal influence.*

If there were an alternative way of funding radio and television stations in order to avoid government influence, that would be desirable. But I think that we need to draw upon public money, which as I said before is our tax money which we deserve to use for good purposes. What remains then to be done is to engage in a continual struggle to see to it that that tax money is unencumbered by censorship.

DB *Another major trend to make up the shortfall of public funding is what was once called "underwriting" and is now called "enhanced underwriting." Some call it outright commercials on public radio and TV. For example, Archer Daniels Midland, "supermarket to the world," is I think the number one underwriter and commercial presence on public radio and TV. Might those kinds of major U.S. corporations, Exxon, IBM, AT&T and others, have an influence on the content of the reporting?*

I don't doubt it. What has happened is that it started with a very tiny mention of somebody who was helping out with a donation. Then these little expressions of gratitude became more and more lavish. The amount of time they were giving to these donors was greater and greater, until these expressions of gratitude began to rival the commercials that you get on ordinary radio and television. It has become kind of ludicrous when you tune in on public radio and you hear some seven different products from seven different companies advertised in the introduction of one program.

DB *A number of award-winning documentaries that could be seen as "controversial" have not been broadcast on PBS, like* The Panama Deception *and* Manufacturing Consent, *which was about Chomsky and an analysis of the media.*

Documentary filmmakers know very well how hard it is to get on television a documentary that is sharply critical of American foreign or domestic policy. I've heard this from many, many filmmakers. A former student of mine, B.J. Bullert, wrote a book about exactly this problem. The book describes the troubles that beset documentary filmmakers when they move outside of political orthodoxy and the difficulty they have of getting on the air. She did a beautiful job in documenting instance after instance in which this was true. Michael Moore is an example. He managed only a few times to get his very funny critiques of the industrial system onto television.

DB *That was* TV Nation. *That was on a commercial network.*

That was on a commercial network. It was cut off. I don't know if his work has been shown on public television.

DB *His famous documentary,* Roger and Me, *was shown on PBS through the P.O.V. series. Let's talk a bit about propaganda. Is it too charged a word to describe the U.S. media?*

Of course it is charged. We tend in the U.S. to resist using that word because we've always associated it with totalitarian states. Yet I think it's a fair word to describe a situation in which the media have some connection with the government, are influenced by the government, have a very strong connection with American corporations, whether directly on commercial television and a little less directly on public radio and television. Where the media generally tend to be nationalistic and patriotic and become unanimous in their support of military operations, then it's fair to say that they're engaging in propaganda. Where they ignore, as they do steadfastly, the dissident activities of groups in the U.S., the meetings that take place of people who belong to environmental or feminist or anti-military groups, I think that deserves to be labeled a kind of active propaganda. Propaganda is not just an act of commission, it's an act of omission.

DB *In* Declarations of Independence, *you write, "If those in charge of our society—politicians, corporate executives, and owners of press and television—can dominate our ideas, they will be secure in their power. They will not need soldiers patrolling the streets. We will control ourselves." What are you getting at there?*

I guess I'm getting at the ingeniousness of the American political and cultural system, an ingeniousness which enables it to hold its military power and police power in reserve for special occasions, groups and events. It doesn't require wholesale police control of the entire population all the time. It can allow apertures for people to express themselves so long as those apertures don't become too great. It can afford to do this, to keep force in reserve, because by controlling our means of communication, our educational system, by keeping watch on what is done on the radio and television and the newspapers and the textbooks of our schools, it can control the information that people have and create a mindset among a majority of the American people which then doesn't require the harsh control of police or military. If it can persuade, for instance by teaching the history of our country in a way that exalts our military heroes and makes our wars just and defensible, if it can create a population which is ready to accept the notion that any time the U.S. sends troops abroad it's for a good purpose, then it doesn't need wholesale jailings of dissidents. It can reserve that force, the military, the courts, for a relatively small number of people who have not been won over by the general indoctrination of the public.

DB *Chomsky and Herman, in their book* Manufacturing Consent, *write, "Institutional critiques are commonly dismissed by establishment commentators as 'conspiracy theories.'"*

I suppose that's a very neat way of simply setting aside anything which is a critique of the system as a whole, any fundamental critique. The system is willing to accept superficial critiques of this policy or that policy but not willing to accept a critique of the capitalist system, of the military system in depth. Suppose somebody does say the problem is not simply electing another President or having a new law. That the problem is the corporate control of the wealth of this country and that the issue is how to change that into economic democracy. When someone begins to talk that way, instead of meeting the argument, meeting the analysis by trying to describe the system in such a way as to persuade people it's a good system, the best way to dispose of that critique is to characterize the argument by saying: You think a small group of people have gotten together and conspired. The reason that opponents of fundamental critiques fasten upon them as conspiracy theory is that conspiracy is immediately seen by most people as not plausible. Most people's common sense will tell them that the things that happen in a society do not happen because five people got into a room and planned it. The conspiracy argument is used against Noam again and again. And again and again he has to say, No, I'm not arguing conspiracy, I'm arguing that there's something systematic that operates which produces the same results over and over again. I suppose that's one of the reasons they don't want to put him on the air. They can make whatever claims they want about his theories without facing sensible arguments.

DB *Social critic and political writer Michael Parenti says about this issue, Of course they meet in rooms. The National Security Council meets in a room. Do you think they meet on a roller coaster on Coney Island?*

I think they meet on a roller coaster on Coney Island. Of course people do meet in rooms. But the fact is, they don't have to work out every detail of what the system does. They will meet in rooms to discuss specific policies. But their coming together in rooms is part of a larger set of events which persistently come out of a system of capitalism, a system where the market, profit and corporate control decide. People will come together in rooms many times, as the National Security Council does. But it's not necessary for them to decide everything that happens. It's not even necessary for them to discuss long-term goals of the system, because the long-term goals of the system are ongoing and perpetuated every day and every hour by the small decisions that are made within the framework of that system.

DB *What then do you think of notions like "media reform," given what you are saying about the capitalist economic structures, the impulse and drive for profit? Can one talk about media reform, as some do, without talking about general economic transformation?*

I think we have to talk about both, just as in the society at large we have to talk about reforms in the economic system, health care, social security, minimum wages, day care. Let's talk about that, because those are more possibly realizable in the short term. Those are things around which you can organize people. At the same time, we need to point out that these reforms will not solve fundamental problems, and that ultimately we will need more basic changes in the system so that we don't have to keep fighting uphill again and again for small changes.

DB *Given what you said earlier about the genius of capitalism to adopt and adapt and to coopt dissent, there will be cosmetic offerings to ameliorate any kind of opposition.*

I didn't use the word "genius," but I did use the word "ingenuity." The ingenuity of the system. And there again it's not a conspiratorial ingenuity. It's not that five people got together in a room and decided this is the way it's going to work, but they act on the basis of their immediate and long-term needs. The Founding Fathers did get together in a room. Michael Parenti is right. They did not get together on a roller coaster on Coney Island. They got together in a room in Philadelphia. They decided to satisfy their immediate needs for control of a possibly rebellious population, for control of possibly rebellious black slaves and Native Americans. They had to satisfy that immediate need by creating a constitutional structure that would set up a strong central government able to deal with rebellion and which would be flexible enough to allow for reform and change by allowing at that time at least a limited franchise. Then, although the Founding Fathers did not foresee this, their successors, that is, the people who became legislators after the Founding Fathers, again and again saw fit to enlarge the franchise and to give people certain political rights and in this way to appease their need for change while at the same time limiting the scope of that change.

DB *You write about the Founding Fathers in* A People's History of the United States *in several chapters. In particular you discuss Shay's*

Rebellion in western Massachusetts in late 1786, which had a very powerful impact on the framers slated to meet in Philadelphia the next year.

Shay's Rebellion was a series of uprisings by farmers, many of them veterans of the American Revolution. They were being beset by taxes levied on them by the general assembly of Massachusetts. The legislature was dominated by merchants and people of wealth, as legislatures generally are almost everywhere. They were levying taxes on these people which they could not afford to pay. They were falling behind in their payments. This is what happens when people fail to pay their taxes: the sheriff arrives with a writ summoning them to appear before a court and then the judge, because they failed to pay their taxes, puts up their farm for sale, as well as their land, their livestock, their possessions. This procedure of foreclosure, of evictions, seizure of property was taking place all over western Massachusetts. These farmers were not able to pay their taxes. Daniel Shays, who had been a captain in the American Revolution, became a leader of a movement to stop this. The movement consisted of armed farmers gathering before courthouses where the foreclosure proceedings were to take place and stopping these procedures from happening. A very direct, forceful, rebellious action. There were times when they would appear and block the judge from entering the courthouse. The sheriff would appear and the sheriff's deputies and they would be greatly outnumbered by the crowd. The sheriff would then call upon the local militia. The local militia would arrive and be sympathetic to the farmers. Sometimes the judge would say, Let's take a vote among the militia to see whether they want us to do this thing. They would take a vote and it would turn out that the militia would be on the side of the farmers.

You might say there was a disruption of the normal order of things in which poor people are simply deprived of their possessions because they aren't able to pay taxes. This is rebellion, revolution. This cannot be tolerated in a society that wants to maintain control and maintain the existing arrangements of property as they have been. Finally an army was put together.

DB   *Led by Hamilton?*

Hamilton was an important figure at this time in all of this, but the army that was raised was led by General Lincoln. It was financed by the merchants of Massachusetts, not by the legislature. Private merchants gathered money to pay for the army. This has happened a number of times in American history, that governments have been unable to pay for the armed forces and the rich have paid because the armed forces were going to do their bidding. The army in this case routed the rebels and defeated them. Many of them, including Shays, left the state and went to Vermont. A few were hanged. The rebellion was crushed. However, it set off great tremors among the leaders of the colonies, who at this time were bound together in the Articles of Confederation, a loose bonding in which the states had a great deal of power. There was no strong central government which could raise an army and collect taxes and create a national treasury. So Shays' Rebellion persuaded a number of people who became the Founding Fathers that a strong central government was needed to control such rebellions in the future. There's a letter that General Knox, who had been a general in the Revolutionary War serving under Washington, wrote to George Washington in which he talked about the dangers of such rebellions. He said, These people want to equalize property. These people are envious of those who are rich and own a lot of property. Letters like this circulated back and forth. The Founding Fathers were even writing to Jefferson, who was in Paris at the time, saying, Look what's happening. Jefferson, being far from the scene and not as alarmed as they were, wrote back and said, Don't worry, a little rebellion now and then is a good thing.

DB *Jefferson said, "The tree of liberty must be refreshed from time to time with the blood of patriots and tyrants. It is its natural manure." Do you know that this has been picked up by right-wing militias in the U.S. today?*

I don't doubt it. Jefferson was giving a rationale for rebellion. People on the left will use it, and they have, and people on the right will use it. In this specific instance, it was the conservative members of the colonial elite, now free from England, who decided that they must convene and amend the Articles of Confederation. That's what the Constitutional Convention originally set out to do, amend the Articles of Confederation. What they did was to then draw up a new Constitution setting up a government which would be strong enough, because it could raise taxes and raise an army, to deal with rebellions like this in the future.

DB *You write, "In New York, where debate over ratification was intense, a series of newspaper articles appeared, anonymously, and they tell us much about the nature of the Constitution. These articles, favoring adoption of the Constitution, were written by James Madison, Alexander Hamilton, and John Jay, and came to be known as the* Federalist Papers." *What do the* Federalist Papers *tell us about the Constitution? You specifically discuss* Federalist Papers #10 *and* #63.

Federalist Paper #10 is probably the most important of all of these eighty-five articles that appeared in the New York newspapers. It was written by James Madison, who was a theoretician, a constitutional scholar. Madison lays out what is probably the fundamental political theory of the American system. He's arguing on behalf of adoption of this Constitution. But in doing so, he's not just giving immediate reasons. He's laying out a theoretical framework. He goes back as the Greeks did, as Aristotle did, in discussing the nature of societies, of politics. He talks about how societies inevitably have factions. These factions are based on who has property and who doesn't have property. There's going to be conflict among these factions on the basis of the owners of property and the non-owners of property. Therefore you need a government to control this conflict between factions. He talked about a majority and a minority faction. He said minority factions can be controlled by setting up a government in which the majority rule. A minority can be more easily controlled by such a government. But a majority faction is something to worry about. That's interesting, because we normally associate democracy with majorities. But he worries about a majority faction. Then he describes what would be the demands of a majority faction that a government would have to worry about. He says you might have "A rage for paper money," "for an equal division of property." He was talking about the fact that at that time poor farmers who were in debt wanted the state governments to issue paper money to make it easy for them to pay their debt, so anybody who was for paper money was going to be against the rich. It goes down to the present day, when the head of the Federal Reserve system says we must not have inflation because inflation will help the debtors, whereas the creditors, the bondholders do not want inflation. It's interesting that there's this continuous thread that runs from the Founding Fathers to the present-day bondholders in the American system. Madison says with these people in the majority faction there will be "A rage for paper money, for an abolition of debts, for an equal division of property, or for any other improper or wicked project." The idea is that this government will be able to control that. This is a very blunt, honest statement about what this government is being set up to prevent, a change in the property arrangements of the society, a change in the distribution of wealth.

DB *Hamilton wrote elsewhere in the* Federalist Papers *that the new Union would be able "to repress domestic faction and insurrection." He referred directly to Shays' Rebellion and continued, "The tempestuous situation from which Massachusetts has scarcely emerged evinces that dangers of this kind are not merely speculative." So they were looking at the real world.*

Oh, yes. You will find in the history books that students get in our schools, at any level, high school, college, university, you will almost never see any connection made as blunt as made by Alexander Hamilton. You will rarely see *Federalist Paper #10* singled out in this way as showing the aim of the American constitutional system as being the maintenance of the present distribution of wealth.

DB *John Jay, one of those framers, apparently was wont to say that "The people who own the country ought to govern it."*

The people who have the wealth should run it. Alexander Hamilton made that statement again and again. It only made sense that the people with the wealth were the people who deserved to run the country.

DB *Why did you write about* Federalist Paper #63?

That's the one that talks about how a legislative body, a "well-constructed Senate," as I recall the phrase, would be able to be a check on what might be the temporary delusions, the temporary impetuous desires of the people. The temper of a representative body would correct the impulses of the population at large. They would be sober and careful. What was being said was that the idea of representative government is not really to represent the will of the people but to calm the anger of the people and to take the wishes of the people, which may be in any one instance powerful and angry, and subject them to the moderating influence of a representative body, to cool the passions of the multitude, to filter them through this representative body. This tells a lot about what is really the aim of representative government.

DB   *I note that you titled this chapter "A Kind of Revolution," not "A Revolution."*

Because if it were a real revolution it would replace the elite control of the colonies by Britain with democratic control by the colonists themselves. Instead, while being somewhat revolutionary in that it gets rid of the British elite, it replaces them with a domestic one. This certainly was recognized more clearly by black people, slaves, who saw that yes, the British had gone but slavery was still here. Slavery was not only here but was legitimized by this Constitution that was just drawn up by the Founding Fathers. And Native Americans, who see in this document the creation of a government which is going to let the colonists loose upon the West and upon Indian territories.

DB   *In the Declaration of Independence, one of the charges against King George is that he released the "merciless savages" upon the hapless colonists.*

The Declaration of Independence is a marvelous expression of the democratic idea that governments are instituted by the people and should be in the interests of the people. There are these things in the Declaration which are embarrassing for democracy today, and that certainly is one of them.

DB   *What were the British up to in 1763 when they declared that a significant portion of North America would remain in Indian hands?*

The British had just finished fighting a war with the French. In that war the Indians had mostly sided with the French. The French had treated the Indians differently than the English had. The French had been willing to assimilate with Indians, whereas the English were conquerors. So when the French and Indian War ended, it was really the North American version of the Seven Year's War in Europe. The English saw the Indians as very dangerous foes. They decided that they wanted to have less conflict with the Indians and therefore the Proclamation of 1763 said, Let's set a boundary on the western border of the colonies. Let's declare that the colonists are not going to move beyond this boundary because that would create more problems with the Indians and that might endanger our whole colonial enterprise in the Northern Hemisphere. So the Proclamation of 1763 was welcomed by the Indians as a limit on western expansion. Therefore, the advent of the American Revolution, which is, of course, celebrated in this country as a great thing, was certainly not celebrated by the Indians because it meant that now the American colonists had free range to go wherever they wanted because the Proclamation of 1763 was no longer operative.

DB *Were the Founding Fathers elected by any kind of popular vote?*

Very few things were done by popular vote at that time. They were a group of people who were selected by the governing bodies of each of the newly free states, free from England but ruled by legislators who were themselves selected only by people of property. Certainly women and blacks and Native Americans did not have the right to vote. People without property did not have the right to vote. It was a very small electorate selecting legislatures which then picked people to be delegates to this convention.

DB *You write that "The Constitution was a compromise between slaveholding interests of the South and moneyed interests of the North." I'd like you to talk about that. You said that "The South agreed" to this compromise "in return for allowing the trade in slaves to continue for twenty years before being outlawed." Twenty years from 1787 would have been 1817. What happened? How come it was extended until the early 1860s?*

What happened was that the law was ignored, as simple as that, a very common feature of not just the American system but of legal systems everywhere, and that is laws which get in the way of the profit of the people who dominate the society are simply ignored. The restriction on the slave trade was simply ignored. Illegal slave trade continued right through the history of the U.S. right up to the Civil War. Very large numbers of slaves were brought to this country despite the supposed banning.

July 28, 1998

DB *In the August 1998* Progressive *you have an article entitled "The Massacres of History" where you review a number of different events, primarily in American history. You write that you recently learned about the Bay View Massacre in Milwaukee, which occurred on May 5, 1886. What happened in the Bay View section of Milwaukee, and how did you find out about it?*

I found out about this massacre because I was invited by some people in Oshkosh, which is not far from Milwaukee, to attend the 100th commemoration of a strike that took place in Oshkosh in 1898, the paper workers' strike. One of the things that made the strike notable, aside from the fact that it was a strike that lasted a long time, was that at the end of the strike some of the strikers were indicted, which happens very often, and they were defended by Clarence Darrow, who gave one of his usual great speeches to the jury and they were acquitted. While being invited to that, I was also invited the next day to commemorate the Bay View Massacre of 1886, which took place right after the Haymarket event of early May 1886. The Bay View Massacre was a situation where steel workers in this steel mill town just outside of Milwaukee were on strike. The strikers were marching toward the mill and they were simply fired at by the police. A number of them were killed, about seven. It became known at least locally as the Bay View Massacre. I had never run into the story of that. I'd read a lot of labor history and a lot of history generally and never read anything about this massacre.

I had occasion to bring that up when I was invited earlier this year to speak at historic Faneuil Hall in Boston at a symposium on the Boston Massacre of 1770. When they invited me I said to them, You want me to speak about the Boston Massacre. I'll come, so long as I don't have to speak about the Boston Massacre. I'd like to speak about other massacres in American history. To my surprise, they said OK. My point was that the Boston Massacre is much celebrated and known to schoolkids who learn about the American Revolution. They almost always learn about the Boston Massacre. One of the notable things about it was that a black or mulatto worker was killed, Crispus Attucks. I decided to try to make the point at this symposium that while it's very easy to celebrate patriotic events like the Boston

Massacre because the American Revolution is one of the patriotic high moments of American history, there were other massacres, more serious in fact, that are forgotten, ignored in the telling of American history. The Bay View Massacre was just one of them.

DB *In that article you ask, for example, why are there not symposia on things that could be called Taino Massacre or the Pequot Massacre.*

The massacre of the Taino Indians on Hispaniola by Columbus and the other *conquistadores* was a far more serious event certainly in terms of the human toll than the Boston Massacre. It was the killing of hundreds of thousands of people, a genocide, really, accompanied by torture and mutilation and starvation and overwork in the mines to the point where the indigenous population of Hispaniola, the island which is now Haiti and the Dominican Republic, was wiped out in a very short time, something that Harvard historian Samuel Eliot Morison called genocide. For him to call it genocide, considering that he was an admirer of Columbus, is quite a remarkable admission.

DB *Let me pose a hypothetical situation to you. What if the German government funded a chair at a major U.S. university, let's say Princeton. This chair is dedicated to denying the Holocaust. What might the reaction be?*

I detect something insidious behind that question. Obviously there would be shock and horror all around. But of course we have chairs commemorating perpetrators of massacre, genocide. The genocide of Columbus was part of a general murder of the indigenous population which certainly rivaled the genocide of Hitler. We don't want to minimize Hitler's Holocaust, but it was not the only act of genocide in history. What happened to the indigenous people here was equivalent. Yet of course cities all over the U.S. have been named after Columbus. Columbia University, my alma mater, named after Columbus. All the celebrations of Columbus on Columbus Day and the huge monument placed in what is now called Columbus Circle in Manhattan. Taking off from what you said, if somebody had proposed statues to Goering everywhere and would have cities named Goeringville, we'd have the equivalent.

DB   *There's an actual case in point. The Turkish government has indeed funded a chair at Princeton. The principal function of this chair is to deny what is called the first genocide of the twentieth century, that of the Armenians in 1915.*

I should say that I'm shocked at Princeton, but of course I'm not. The Ivy League universities are as complicit in the distortion of history and in the celebration of murder as any other institution except that it comes as even more of a troubling point because of the pretense of institutions like Princeton and Harvard and the others to be institutions of higher education.

DB   *Why, for example, in the general discourse, is not the genocide of the Armenians very well known, in spite of an enormous amount of archival evidence in the U.S., Britain, France, Germany and Turkey, eye-witness reports, newspapers accounts of the time? It's not on most people's radar screens.*

I can think of a couple of reasons. One is that there are not enough Armenians in the U.S. to vote a Congressman out of office or to make a significant difference in the election of a President. But also I think there is another reason: the long-term connection of the U.S. with the Turkish government, a connection based on a military alliance with the Turkish military dictatorship for a long period of time. It's an old story in American foreign policy that the U.S. has allied itself with military dictatorships all over the world, overlooking the terrible things they did to their own people. What we are saying now about our alliance with Turkey and therefore our tendency to overlook what the Turks did to the Armenians in 1915 is comparable with our military alliance with Suharto in Indonesia and overlooking the massacre of the people in East Timor.

DB   *Indeed, efforts to get any kind of Congressional recognition of this event, not saying anything about it but just acknowledging it, have been squashed.*

Congress has not been known for its moral perception in passing resolutions and legislation, so I'm not really surprised.

DB *Apparently Hitler was aware of what happened to the Armenians and the fact that there was no justice rendered after the genocide. In a meeting with his generals just days before the invasion of Poland in 1939, he asked rhetorically, "Who today speaks of the extermination of the Armenians?" He was kind of inspired by what had happened.*

That's interesting. I guess people who are prepared to commit heinous crimes and perhaps are cautioned by somebody outside or internally about what might be the consequences of these can simply point to all the instances in history where atrocities have taken place and nothing has happened to those who committed them.

DB *Talk about lamenting. You comment in* A People's History: *"My point is not to grieve for the victims and denounce the executioners. Those tears, that anger, cast into the past, deplete our moral energy for the present." I'm interested in this depletion of moral energy for the present.*

I was trying to make the point that it is very easy to become emotionally wrought up about something that happened in the past. But if it is not carried over into the present, if it doesn't become a starting point for moral indignation for things that are happening today, then there's an enormous waste of moral energy. The World War II Holocaust is an example. We've had an enormous amount of grieving over the Holocaust, and of course it deserves grieving over. But on the other hand, too much of that grieving has come as an exercise in remembering the past while blocking recognition of things that are happening in the present. I think of Elie Wiesel, who has spent so much of his literary talent dealing with the Holocaust. Yet I don't remember him speaking out on the war in Vietnam. I don't remember him speaking out against what is happening to the Palestinians in Israel. I remember once I was asked to participate in a program sponsored by Hillel House at Boston University to talk about the Holocaust. I suppose in a sense I was doing there what I did later with the Boston Massacre. I said, Let's go beyond that. Let's look at other holocausts. Otherwise, a simple remembrance of the 1940s holocaust will be of no moral value. So I talked mostly about the atrocities that were going on at that time in Central America, which the U.S. was not only overlooking but abetting by giving military aid to the military governments of El Salvador and Guatemala, giving aid to the *contras*. The U.S. was in effect responsible in the way that the people who were put on trial in Nuremberg were responsible for genocide even though they didn't actually release the gas from the chambers. The U.S. was responsible for the deaths of several hundred thousand people in Central America. So that was the gist of my talk. After that there was an angry response by a man in the audience who was a survivor of the Holocaust. He was angry because I departed from the Holocaust to talk about other things. He wanted me only to concentrate on that. To me, that concentration on a past event to the exclusion of present atrocities is an empty exercise in sentimental remembering and a moral failure.

DB *You're Jewish. To what extent do Judaism and Jewish culture inform your intellectual development?*

I wish I knew. Shall I respond in Yiddish? A couple of months ago—I always answer these questions by going far afield, and then perhaps I come back to answer the question, it's a Jewish trait—I got a letter from a young man on the West Coast, a student who said he'd been reading my memoir, *You Can't Be Neutral on a Moving Train,* and he liked it very much. But, he said, I noticed that you just passed very lightly over your Jewishness. You don't say anything about how your Jewish background affected your values. It took me a while to answer him. It's hard to answer that question, just like it's hard to answer your question. On the one hand, I have no doubt that growing up Jewish and being aware of being Jewish, being aware of what Jews have suffered in the past and being aware even in the present of the anti-Semitism still in the world, and also growing up in the era of fascism and Hitler, inevitably had an effect on my sensitivity towards oppression and racism. It's wrong for me to say growing up Jewish meant nothing to me. On the other hand, I don't want to overemphasize the effect of growing up Jewish on the development of my attitudes towards war and peace and racism and justice because it's obvious to anyone who thinks about it that there are Jews who grew up with the same kind of Jewish heritage that I did who ended up supporting, as Kissinger did, mass murder in Southeast Asia and in Indonesia. There are Jews on both sides of the political boundary. On the other hand, I've found in my life that so many of the people who have shared exactly the same values that I have are people who did not grow up Jewish, people from all sorts of backgrounds. Armenians, for instance, but also American Anglo-Saxons. I mentioned earlier and in my memoirs write about Staughton Lynd, who was a colleague of mine who comes from a very different background from mine. But he ended up with the same values I did.

DB *A central myth of Zionism is "a land without people for a people without a land." Does that have historical antecedents with other views of empty spaces, perhaps peopled by a few primitives?*

I have a hunch with your delicately pointed questions that you know the answer but you might be talking about the invasion of North America by Europeans into presumably an empty continent. You can say the North Americans did to the so-called empty continent what Israel did to Palestine. They turned this desert into a flowering garden, except that of course the so-called desert was peopled by human beings, and these human beings were simply overlooked. I remember when I went to school, probably in junior high school, learning about the Louisiana Purchase, when the U.S. in 1803 purchased this enormous territory from the Mississippi River to the Rockies, a huge part of what is now the U.S. I remember getting the impression that this was simply empty territory and what a wonderful thing that we now had this empty territory and could do with it what we wanted. I was not told anything about the huge number of native tribes that lived in this area and how the acquisition of the Louisiana Territory meant the extermination of these Indian tribes in order to make that land ready for Europeans to settle.

DB *In a talk you gave in Cambridge in late June 1998, you pointed to euphemistic terms like the Louisiana Purchase, the Florida Purchase and the Mexican Cession. Wasn't it wonderful that Mexico just ceded all this territory to the growing U.S.?*

It was all represented in classrooms by these lovely maps on the wall with different colors representing the different acquisitions. It was all called "Westward Expansion," the word "expansion" suggesting some sort of biological kind of process, benign, non-violent. The terms Mexican Cession and Florida Purchase were euphemisms for very violent forays into other areas. In the case of Florida, Andrew Jackson led military expeditions into Florida, killing people, and then Spain, in presumably a benign commercial action, "sells" Florida to the U.S.

The Mexican Cession or war, was instigated by the U.S. in order to take half of Mexico, what is now the entire Southwest part of the U.S., including California. I wonder how many schoolkids in California growing up know that the territory they are on belonged to Mexico. I wonder how the Californians who now rage against Mexicans coming into California know that this once belonged to Mexico and it was the Yankees who invaded California and took it away.

DB   *You've said that George Orwell is one of your favorite writers. He wrote an essay that talks about the use of language, euphemisms, question-begging, called "Politics and the English Language." One of the terms he discusses is "pacification."*

"Pacification" is a nice word. It suggests that you're bringing peace to a warlike situation. We've had a very recent experience of pacification, and that is in the Vietnam War, where "pacification" meant the destruction of villages. I suppose it's true that when you kill somebody you pacify them. They can no longer speak, they can no longer react, they can no longer do anything, they are "peaceful" in death. The term pacification has been used by the British in building the British Empire, through a series of violent wars by the Americans, not just recently in Vietnam but before that in the Philippines.

DB   *In several talks you've referred to Emile Zola's* Germinal, *a film adaptation of his novel about mine workers in the nineteenth century. In particular you mention a* Boston Globe *review that attracted your attention. What drew you to that?*

It just jumped out at me. I go to the movies. I read reviews. I had read the novel *Germinal* years ago. I was a fan of Zola because like Dickens he was a naturalist. He wrote in the most gripping terms about the reality that poor people faced. So when I saw that a movie had been made about his novel, I was very interested. The review was a rather negative one. It didn't get the kind of rave review that a movie like *Get Shorty* or any movie today depicting violence receives. This was too serious a movie for the reviewer and he didn't like it. But what struck me particularly was the end of the review, where they usually give the designation as good for children, PG, or R for restricted. When a movie is designated R it's usually because there's violence and/or nudity. I noticed that *Germinal* got the designation R. Then they usually describe why that designation is given. I expected to see nudity, violence, but no. The explanation for the R was, "depiction of intense suffering and class conflict." That jumped out at me. It was such a perfect illustration of how American culture rejects the notion of class conflict, when in fact of course our history has been absolutely loaded with class conflict from the very beginning.

DB *You'll be happy or unhappy to know that the tradition continues at the* Boston Globe. *Its July 26, 1998 review of the film* The Mask of Zorro, *about the Spanish swashbuckler, gave it a PG rating. It must be profanity and violence. No. Viewers are warned of "peasants enslaved at mine."*

I didn't see that review. Thanks for calling it to my attention. I will use it for the next ten years.

DB *Speaking of the venerable* Boston Globe, *now owned by the New York Times, you had a journalistic kind of period in the mid-1970s writing op-ed pieces. Some of them have been reprinted in* The Zinn Reader. *What was that like for you in terms of writing in short form, very limited space, not a lot of room for detail and explication.*

I liked it. When I was a kid I thought of being a journalist. I liked the idea of writing something that's concise. I've never really wanted to write long, scholarly articles. It was an opportunity for me to reach a large audience with short essays. I think it's fair to say that the op-ed pieces I wrote for the *Globe*, which was for about a year and a half, were very important to me. They certainly were different from other material people were getting in there. My co-columnist, we alternated columns, was Eric Mann, a young Boston radical at that time. Now he's a somewhat older California radical, organizing people on the West Coast. I think the *Globe* labeled our column "Left Field Notes," or something like that, just so people would know that that's what we represented and be warned in advance. I don't want to impute too much malice to that kind of title. That lasted for about a year and a half.

DB *You note that the liberalism of the* Globe *"had its limits." What happened?*

My column came abruptly to an end. Eric Mann's column came abruptly to an end a little before mine. I remember one time both of us went to the *Globe* to protest because they had tried to censor a column that Eric Mann wrote about Israel, which was critical of Israel's policy. Other than that we had experienced no censorship. But on Memorial Day 1976, I wrote a column which was, I guess, not the traditional Memorial Day column exalting and remembering in fond ways the wars and the soldiers who fought in the wars. It was a Memorial Day column which said we should celebrate Memorial Day by making up our minds never to have another war, never to have any more veterans, never to have any more bodies come home in plastic bags. Perhaps we should use Memorial Day to celebrate those people who had acted against war, people who had refused to go to war. That was my last column. After that my column just disappeared, without explanation.

DB *You never got a pink slip in the mail?*

Never got any colored slip in the mail. No explanation. In order to get an explanation I had to ask for one. When I asked for it they said, We have a new editor for the editorial page who thinks perhaps there are too many political columns on the op-ed page. Very strange statement. By the early seventies protest became somewhat respectable. By this time the nation had acknowledged that the protesters had played some part in stopping the war in Vietnam. I think it was in that spirit that the *Boston Globe* invited me and Eric Mann to do a column. By 1976 that aura had worn off. Maybe this was the beginning of trying to do away with the Vietnam syndrome.

DB *Talk about the use of the passive voice versus the active voice. Orwell writes about this in "Politics and the English Language" as well. I notice in* A People's History, *for example, you write, "The English landed and killed some Indians. The English went from one deserted village to the next, destroying crops." You could have just as easily written that "Indians were killed" and "crops were destroyed." Why did you choose the active voice?*

I'd like to say that I had read Orwell just the day before and deliberately chose the active voice, but I think I just naturally, unconsciously used it because it seemed a stronger and more accurate way of stating what some people did to others in the course of history. As Orwell pointed out, it does make a difference whether you use the active or the passive voice in giving power to whatever you say.

DB *And defining agency, perhaps?*

Defining who does what to whom.

DB *A recent example of this passive voice construction was in a* New York Times *editorial. They wrote about the 1965 period in Indonesia, when "half a million people on the country's political left were murdered." That was enlightening. One doesn't find out who did the murdering.*

The use of passive voice in that case always implies an act of God. Something happened to people and we're not going to emphasize who was responsible. That's a good example.

DB *Let's talk about* A People's History of the United States. *When did you start writing it?*

I thought about writing it I suppose at the end of the Vietnam War, when I found myself with a little more free time. It was around 1977 that I signed a contract with Harper & Row, now HarperCollins, pushed to do it by two people, my agent, Rick Balkin, and my wife Roslyn. I went to Paris in 1978 for a four-month professorship, thinking that like all those famous writers who went to Paris to write, I would do the same. I brought my notes that I had gathered with me so that I could begin writing A People's History in Paris during that four-month stay. I didn't write a word. Paris was too much. So I returned to the U.S., where I went to work in 1978, finished in 1979. It took less than a year to write A People's History, which surprises people and sometimes makes them think I obviously did it in a hurry and didn't spend much time on it. But of course I'd been accumulating the notes and material, the data, for twenty years as a result of teaching and writing about history. So I had an enormous amount of material at hand. Once I sat down to write, I didn't use a computer yet, I had my old manual typewriter, it came very fast. I wrote very intensely and stayed up into the wee hours of every morning.

DB *Was that on that Underwood Number 5 that your parents gave you?*

It would be very romantic for me to say that, but I cannot tell a lie. It was a Royal. My Underwood Number 5 I had given to my daughter when she went off to college. It was very close to the Underwood. It behaved the same way.

DB *In the course of your investigations in writing* A People's History, *what facts came out that were startling to you?*

I suppose just as the reader of my *People's History* were startled by my story of Columbus, I was startled myself. I must confess that until I began looking into it, I did not know any more about Columbus than I had learned in school. By this time I had a Ph.D. in American history. Nothing that I learned on any level of education, from elementary school through Columbia University, changed the story of the heroic Columbus and his wonderful accomplishments. It wasn't until I began to look into it myself, read Columbus' journals, read Las Casas, the great eyewitness who produced many volumes on what happened to the Indians, not until I began to read did I suddenly realize with a kind of shock how ignorant I had been and with another shock how ignorant I had been led to be by the education I had gotten in our national education system.

DB *What about your methodology? How did you go about your task? Was it chronologically disciplined?*

At first my idea was to organize the book according to topics and issues. I thought I'd have a section on race and would carry the section on race right from the first slaves brought to Jamestown down through the present, do the same thing with labor, and so on. Then I discarded that idea. I thought I would use a more traditional approach and deal in rough chronological form with the topics that are dealt with in the orthodox American textbooks. Then it would be more obvious that I was dealing with the same topics but from a completely different point of view, and also my book would be more useful to teachers. Students could look at my book parallel to other books, go through the same chronology and find a completely different version of the events.

DB *I'm interested stylistically in what you did at the very beginning of the book. With Columbus disembarking on an island in the Caribbean and you're embarking on your journey. So as Columbus arrives, Zinn takes off.*

It's very nice of you to pair me with Columbus. Do you think I may have statues named after me as a result? I never thought of it that way. One thing about my methodology is that I resisted the idea of an introduction or foreword or preface. I jumped right in with the very first sentence, describing Columbus' arrival. Because I thought that dramatically it would be more interesting to jump right into the story. I've always had a certain resentment against forewords and prefaces and introductions. They always got in the way of the story. Yet editors still, there's a kind of traditional wisdom among editors, which I think is very much misplaced, think it's important to have a preface or introduction. I began the story before discussing my general approach to history. The traditional approach would be, Let me discuss my general approach to history and then go into the story, but I get ten or twelve pages into the story and then I stop and say, Here's my approach to history and move on.

DB *I found that technique artistically also very interesting and compelling. It has a kind of electronic parallel in radio and TV programs, for example, there's a tease at the top and then the announcer comes on and back-announces it.*

I'm sure they got it from me.

DB *You do that kind of back-announcing. You talk about Samuel Eliot Morison and what you're trying to do in terms of writing a new history from the perspective of the human impact of history on people. You also cite Henry Kissinger in his first book,* A World Restored, *in which he writes that "history is the memory of states."*

Kissinger has always been one of my favorites. I was not surprised when I read that in his book, which is actually his doctoral dissertation. It was an exact representation of Kissinger's Machiavellian view of history. That is, you look at history and the world from the standpoint, as Machiavelli did, of the Prince. Kissinger looks at it from the standpoint of Nixon, the President or the President's advisors. My book was intended to do exactly the opposite, to look at history from the standpoint of those people who were victims of the state, those ordinary people who are not the people in power. When you look at the world from the viewpoint of the state, as Kissinger does, everything looks different. Then you can, as he did, look at the nineteenth century as an era of peace, as the great states were not at war with one another as they would be shortly thereafter in World War I. Very often that era, from 1815, the Congress of Vienna, is seen as a time when the great powers got together and established a kind of, yes, peace until 1914. From the point of view of the states, there was peace. From the point of view of ordinary people there was no peace. During that period those states were marauding in the world, conquering the Middle East and Asia. In the case of the U.S., it was conquering Latin America. Internally during that period those states were collaborating with the exploitation of their working classes by the rising industries of that time. So those are two very, very different points of view about history.

DB *In the July 27, 1998* Boston Globe *there's a full-page ad announcing "Success 1998, Massachusetts' Most Popular Business Seminar." "How much you earn is determined by how much you learn. Attend this dynamic seminar and learn the latest strategies for business and personal success." Kissinger is among those who will be speaking. He is described here as someone who has "earned his place in history as the most influential leader in foreign policy of our generation, as Secretary of State and member of the President's Foreign Intelligence Advisory Board, he established himself as a respected peacemaker and healer of complex international crises."*

I'd like to know who wrote that. Is that part of the ad?

DB *It's a kind of bio, a hook to get you to attend.*

So it wasn't a *Globe* writer, it was part of the advertisement. People who write advertisements have absolutely no connection with truth telling. They're selling something. Here they are selling this seminar, I guess, for which people pay a lot of money. In the course of it they don't care how much they lie. Talking about Kissinger as a peacemaker is certainly a gross misstatement of history. Here is a man who was one of the architects and advisors to the continuing war in Vietnam, to the bombing of Cambodia to the killing of several million people in Southeast Asia, and to call him a "peacemaker" is absurd. It's interesting that they're talking about education here. The people who wrote this are very badly educated.

DB *How is it that personages, like Kissinger, who "earned their place in history," can sit with someone like Richard Nixon and say nothing in the face of what is now universally acknowledged as Nixon's raving anti-Semitism?*

Kissinger was the master opportunist. That advertisement wouldn't say that in describing him. Nixon's anti-Semitism did not obviously mean as much to Kissinger as the fact that Nixon had made Kissinger his close advisor. Such a terrible example of groveling before power, certainly a shameful thing for a Jew, after Jews had been the victims of power and after Jews had watched other people grovel before power and ignore what was happening to Jews. Kissinger is repeating, in his own person, what Jews have condemned in Pope Pius XII during World War II, condemned in those people who were silent or who collaborated in the victimization of others.

DB *How did these personages get elevated into some kind of pantheon?*

Our pantheons are sculpted by people like Kissinger. It's an inside club in which they all decide that one another are great. That's why you have Theodore Roosevelt sitting up there on Mount Rushmore, although he was a lover of war and a racist, a celebrator of vicious acts against other people.

DB *In A People's History you cite Albert Camus' suggestion about victims and executioners, "It's the job of thinking people not to be on the side of the executioners."*

I was trying to make the point that we who do history, we who are scholars, we who do anything in the world should reject the notion of neutrality. As Camus said, in a world of victims and executioners, you cannot be neutral. You cannot pretend to be objective in such a world. I was suggesting that historians should take the side of the victims and not the side of the executioners.

DB *Various groups over time have claimed, "History is on our side." You write, "I don't want to invent victories for people's movements."*

I wanted to avoid a kind of facile romanticization of the past in which the people win glorious victories. First of all, from a practical point of view, to any thinking person it obviously would be a misrepresentation of reality. But also from the point of view of historical accuracy. After all, history has been dominated by people with wealth and power. The struggles of ordinary people against that have often ended in failure. Sure, there have been successes. But to exaggerate the successes would be to minimize the obstacles that people face in overcoming their situation and creating a different world.

DB *You talk about emphasizing new possibilities by disclosing those hidden episodes of the past.*

I think that one of the worst things about the way history is taught is that it ignores or minimizes those times in history when people who are apparently powerless have gotten together, organized themselves and accomplished remarkable things. For instance, when I was learning about the period of slavery and the Civil War going to school, and again, this is true from elementary school up to graduate school, I was never given a full picture of the anti-slavery movement. The abolitionist movement was an absolutely extraordinary achievement, filled with heroes and heroines, something that would inspire any young person to become a fighter against injustice. We're never given a full picture of that. The person who dominates our history books in terms of the emancipation of slaves is Abraham Lincoln. But there were all of those actions taken by people against slavery. I think for instance of a set of actions that took place in the 1850s, just before the Civil War, after the Fugitive Slave Act was passed in 1850, and when the federal government was collaborating with Southern slave owners to bring escaped slaves back into captivity. People in the North, black people, white people, banded together in what were called vigilante committees. The word "vigilante" had a different connotation then. There were people who were vigilant about what was happening to other people, and when a slave was captured they would invade the courthouse, the police station, they would rescue the slave. They would send the ex-slave on the way to Canada to freedom. They did heroic things. They risked their lives, their freedom, they risked being put in jail. Also, as part of this very inspiring set of episodes, very often when these people were put on trial for abetting the escape of a slave and for interfering with federal authorities, the juries acquitted them. The juries were sympathetic to them, because by the 1850s there had been a building up of the abolitionist movement. A noble period of American history, forgotten moments, lost moments, but those moments should be remembered because they suggest to us what is possible for apparently powerless people to accomplish in the face of overwhelming odds. We've seen that again and again.

DB *Do you think the question, Whose side is history on? is the wrong question?*

There's no real answer to that question. If you answer that question, you will be declaring a determinist view of history, like inevitably history must be on the side of the oppressor or the oppressed. I think history is open. If we think of history as closed I think it depletes our energy. If we think it's closed against us, then we are left in a state of helplessness. If we think it's for us, then we think we don't have that much to do.

DB *After the collapse of the Soviet Union in the early 1990s, Francis Fukuyama proclaimed "the end of history." In an age of capitalist triumphalism and U.S. hegemony, does history have any future?*

I think it does. I don't think it has come to an end. That was wishful thinking on his part. It's a Hegelian notion, really. Hegel also saw history reaching an end at a certain point. Actually, the end being the supremacy of the German state. Fukuyama sees it as the end being the victory of capitalism. It's very clear, and should be clear to him, I hope, that he was speaking too soon. Capitalism has not triumphed. It's true that the Soviet Union has disintegrated, but capitalism has only revealed itself since then more and more as incapable of solving the problems of the world. The intrusion of a capitalist ethic into Russia these past years has been disastrous, leaving many people to harken back romantically even to the era of Stalin. With all of the terrible things that happened under Stalin, people remember that they had jobs, they had food...

DB *Health care...*

It was a welfare state. This very happy export of capitalism to other countries has obviously resulted in disaster. We're a long way from the end of history because we have something very important yet to do. Michael Moore in his latest film, *The Big One*, meaning the United States, has a last line I thought was classic: One evil empire down, one to go.

DB *What role do you see, then, for historians in shaping the future?*

Historians have a responsibility to point out to people several things. It's very important to point out the history of our political institutions, the history of capitalism, the suffering that has gone on under capitalism. It's very important for historians to expose the emptiness of the promises that have been made and the emptiness behind the glorification of past and present institutions. And at the same time to bring back into our view those events in history which show that under certain circumstances, at certain points in history, if they organize, if they risk, if they act together, if they keep an ideal in their minds, it is possible for people to change things.

DB *Who among current historians do you admire?*

In England we just had recently the passing of E.P. Thompson, I think he is one of the most extraordinary of contemporary historians, who wrote the classic work, *The Making of the English Working Class*. To me he was exemplary not just because he was a historian who unearthed the history of class struggle and class conflict and the awakening of working class consciousness in England, but because he acted out his beliefs in his personal life. In his last years he became one of the important voices in England speaking against the nuclear arms race. I see him as a model of a scholar-activist. In this country, there are a number of admirable historians. Staughton Lynd is one of them, although he's not officially a historian. Of course, many of our best historians are not officially historians. He was once, then he became a labor lawyer when he was drummed out of the profession. He and his wife, Alice Lynd, have put together a remarkable compendium of documents of nonviolent resistance in American history, *Nonviolence in America*. To me it is an absolutely essential work. Talking about people who are not officially historians but have done marvelous history, Noam Chomsky comes immediately to mind. He's give us all sorts of history, of the Middle East, Central America, America and foreign relations, history of the last five hundred years of capitalism in the world. I know of no one who is officially a historian who can match him. There are others. Eric Foner has done a great book on the Reconstruction period, the best book that's been written since W.E.B. Du Bois' *Black Reconstruction*. I think of Richard Drinnon, who has written some remarkable books. I mentioned at some other point his biography of Emma Goldman, which affected me greatly, but I also think of his book *Facing West*, a brilliant survey of American expansionism, using the word "expansionism" now in a much more critical way, in this country against the Indians, abroad in Vietnam and against the Philippines, an absolutely remarkable synthesis of history and literature, beautifully written. Drinnon also wrote a very good account of our incarceration of the Japanese in concentration camps during World War II. It is the story of Dillon Myer, the commandant of those concentration camps.

We now have in the U.S. a whole generation of new historians. I think of Gerda Lerner, who has brought to light women's history. I think of Rosalyn Baxandall and Linda Gordon and Susan Reverby who did a book on the history of working women, *America's Working Women*. I shouldn't ignore the Marxist historians who did pioneering work which enabled so many of us to go on from there. Philip Foner. No more prolific historian exists in the U.S. He died a few years ago. Herbert Aptheker, whose *A Documentary History of the Negro People in the U.S.* is still the most valuable single source book for black history. Very often people ask me, Where can I get information? I tell them, Go to the library.

DB *Are you suggesting perhaps with people like Chomsky and Lynd that it's quite possible to be a historian, do valuable historical work, and be "outside" the traditional profession?*

In some ways it's easier. You're not constricted by the requirements of the profession or by the thought that fellow historians are looking over your shoulder making sure that you are "professional." After all, doing history is not like preparing for becoming a neurosurgeon. It doesn't require an enormous amount of very specialized, meticulous training. It requires a basic intelligence, a willingness to look far and wide for sources, and an open mind. Any intelligent person with an independent frame of mind who is willing to work hard in the archives and the libraries can produce great history.

DB *Those archives and libraries are undergoing a radical transformation, as you know. History and cyberspace. Years ago you stumbled upon a file cabinet in New York with LaGuardia's archives and that led to your dissertation and first book. How will electronic communication change the archives of the future? For example, do you see the collected e-mail of some famous figure?*

I think of my collected e-mail, which is already huge. I suppose, I don't like to think of the books and manuscripts being displaced. I still would rather go through the actual crumbling newspapers of the past than look at microfilm. And yet, I think we should make use of whatever modern devices there are that can be helpful. I see the electronic collection of information as being a supplement to the traditional sources, not replacing them.

DB *Do you see any discernible political implications of e-mail and cyberspace?*

I see two different kinds of implications. One is making more information available to more people through the use of the Web. On the other hand, there's also the possibility, as there has been with the other media, of control. It remains to be seen whether the democratic aspect will outweigh the controlling aspect.

DB *Turning to your writing style, which is fluid, fluent, straightforward and direct. I'm wondering to what extent you've been influenced by literature, novels for example. You've mentioned* The Death of Ivan Illich, *by Leo Tolstoy and James Joyce's* A Portrait of the Artist as a Young Man. *We've talked about Dickens and Orwell and others.*

I guess I've always been aware that fiction can often represent history more accurately than non-fiction. As I mentioned in a previous interview, John Steinbeck's *The Grapes of Wrath* can represent the Depression more realistically than a dry set of statistics about how many people were unemployed and how many people were hungry during the 1930s. I've always been aware of that because it has always seemed to me that the representation of reality is not simply a matter of telling about a past event on a flat surface, but that by going beneath that surface and by exploring something in detail and by making it more vivid, by writing about it in a literary way, you are bringing that event to life much more importantly than by a simple prosaic description. So I've always been interested in literature for that reason. When I read Upton Sinclair's novel about the Sacco and Vanzetti case, *Boston*, I had read other things about the case, but I thought, This brings those events into our imagination, into our vision, much more powerfully than any non-fiction account could do, and without doing an injustice to the facts.

DB *How would you feel about inventing facts, So-and-so turned to So-and-so and said this? These are pure fabrications.*

That's something else. When Steinbeck writes about the Depression, you know he's inventing characters, but at the same time you know that these characters are going through real events which may in their details not be exact replicas of actual events, but which suggest very powerfully what those actual events are. I think to invent dialogue, for instance, is probably going too far, unless you're writing a novel. Sometimes dialogue is invented in historical accounts, pretending to know what Jefferson said to Adams. You don't have to pretend. You can actually quote Jefferson's letters to Adams. So I think you have to be careful. The most important thing is honesty. The reader should know whether he or she is reading fact or something imaginatively constructed.

DB *You had something in mind in a lecture when you mentioned Tolstoy's* Death of Ivan Illich *and Joyce's* Portrait of the Artist as a Young Man. *What was that?*

I think what I had in mind was that young people, especially when thinking about their whole future lying ahead of them, should try to imagine what Ivan Illich went through when at the end of his life, Tolstoy is giving young people an opportunity to see forty or fifty years ahead and ask, How will I think back upon my life forty or fifty years from now. For them to see that Ivan Illich, this successful man, this man who did everything right, looks back at his life and says, This is not the kind of life I wanted to lead, is something very instructive for young people, who are being captivated, being pressured on all sides to get money, to get success, to do the right things, all of them superficial, evanescent, the kinds of things that at the end of one's life will evaporate immediately. I very often talk about *The Death of Ivan Illich* because I want young people to think about the question of, What am I living my life for? What can I be proud of when I go? What will my grandchildren be proud of when they think of my life? Similarly with James Joyce, who said, I want to live my life freely. I don't want to be hampered by authority. I want to decide for myself how I want to think and what I want to do.

DB *Clearly, it's too soon to talk about a Zinn legacy, but I was wondering if you could speculate on that.*

I don't think it's too soon to talk about a legacy. I think we should have started talking about it a long time ago, maybe when I was ten years old. A Zinn legacy. What do I leave? I think the best legacy one can leave is people. I can say, I would like to leave a legacy of books, and yes, there are writings that have an effect on people and it's good to think that you've written something that has made people think, and think about their lives. When I say legacy is people, I guess I mean people have been affected by reading, by your life, or people you've encountered. The best kind of legacy you can leave is a kind of example of how one should live one's life, not that I've lived my life in an exemplary way, but let's put it this way, people should be very selective about what they look at in my life. If I were to single out, as I would be prone to do, only the good things, I would think of the necessity to work at changing the world and at the same time maintain a kind of decency towards all the people around you. So that what you are striving for in the future is acted out in the present in your human relations.

DB *Kind of like that New York expression, not just talk the talk, which is convenient, safe and easy, but walk the walk.*

Those New York expressions are OK.

DB *Not only are you a great teller of history, but you are also a wonderful storyteller. I've attended a lot of your public talks and recorded them. You have an enormous ability to convey history in a very user-friendly way. What do you attribute that to? You're very easy to listen to. In the* *course of this interview there's a lot of fluency and facility. In front of large audiences you seem to be relaxed. People feel that. They sense that they're with a friend. They're with somebody who's not lecturing them or lecturing to them but is talking with them.*

I learned early when I began teaching and speaking publicly that it was not good for me to prepare too well, to work out what I was going to say, whether in a classroom or before a public audience. That destroyed the atmosphere of spontaneity and the possibility of responding very immediately to who my audience was and what the situation was. I found it was better when I did that, when I left openings, when I was willing to be interrupted and willing to interrupt myself and willing to pause and think on the platform. There's nothing that scares beginning speakers more than the thought that they will have a moment, or second, with nothing to say. I found that if I was honest, honest meaning, Yes, I really don't know what I'm going to say this next second, I have to think about it, that the audience was with me because they were very often in the same position. They understood that you have to think about what you say. Also, it created a kind of dramatic suspense to have a little pause as you were working out your next thoughts. It just made life easier for me when I discovered that I didn't have to meticulously prepare my lectures.

I'm going to let you in on a secret. I don't tell this to everybody, but when I'm going to give a lecture in Boulder, Colorado, I just picked that city of course out of the blue, I will not do any preparation except that before I get on the plane I will go through my files and quickly pluck out stuff that I think is relevant to the topic that I have said I would talk about, although I usually pick topics with titles so general as to give me a lot of leeway. I will pick stuff out of my files and throw them into my bag. Then on the plane I will rummage through them and let the material percolate in my head and then perhaps write down a very rough outline which in the course of my talk I may not even refer to but which will prepare me in some way. I found that I simply enjoyed talking more and enjoyed teaching more when I didn't have that burden of ultra-careful preparation. It was more fun.

DB *In the mid-1990s you updated* A People's History. *What did you add, and did you subtract or delete anything from the previous body of work?*

I didn't subtract or delete anything, because, as you know, everything I write is precious. It would be an act of cruelty to delete anything that I had written. But I did add because the original edition ended in the 1970s, and I wanted to bring the story up into the 1990s. I had actually gone into the Carter Administration in the 1970s, but I wanted to go into Reagan and Bush. I deliberately wrote a chapter in which I combined my discussion of Carter, Reagan and Bush. I wanted to make the point that, although they differ in detail, in general the policies of the liberal Carter and the conservative Reagan and Bush fell within the framework of American tradition. That tradition is capitalist and nationalist. Carter, even though he was among this triumvirate the liberal of the three, still maintained the military budget and a fundamentally nationalist foreign policy. Carter simply went along with what Indonesia was doing to the people in East Timor. In his domestic policy he did not make any really important changes in the direction of distributing the wealth of the country in a more equitable way. So the class issues and the nationalist issues were dealt with in roughly the same way by these three Presidents. I wanted in that one chapter which I added to make that point. I quoted Richard Hofstadter in *The American Political Tradition*, to me by far the best book that Hofstadter wrote, where he said that as he went through American history, there was a consistent American political tradition based upon nationalism, upon the idea of private property, the latter being a euphemism for capitalism. Then I wanted to also add a chapter on the resistance to the policies of these Presidents. I did a chapter called "The Unreported Resistance." That adjective "unreported" could be applied to resistance throughout American history. But in this particular case I wanted to bring out the fact that for instance the policies of Reagan did not go without opposition throughout the country. Reagan's policies in Central America brought about protests and demonstrations all over the country. Here in Boston we had 550 people sit in at the federal building in Boston to protest against Reagan's declaration of a blockade on Nicaragua. 60,000 people in the country signed a pledge of resistance that if Reagan invaded Nicaragua these people would act in some way against that.

In the early Reagan years there was a great anti-nuclear movement in which several million people participated, calling for a freeze on nuclear arms by the Soviet Union and the U.S. In 1982 there was a huge demonstration, close to a million people, in Central Park in New

York. All over the country, city councils and state legislatures and even Congress passed resolutions calling for a nuclear freeze. Those were also the years when the policy of being nice to the white government of South Africa was opposed on hundreds of college campuses, with rallies that called for the divestment by American corporations and universities of their South African-connected holdings.

Maybe the most vivid example of underreported resistance was what happened in the Bush Administration during the Gulf War, where the impression was given of near-unanimous support of the Gulf War by the American people. I tried in that chapter to tell something of the widespread protests against the Gulf War that took place, even though it was a very short war and there was very little time to organize protests. It was a protest that was much greater than there had been in the early months of the Vietnam War.

DB *How many copies of* A People's History *have been sold?*

About 500,000. The interesting thing about the publication history is that the sales have gone up each year. The usual situation with books is that they sell the greatest number in the first year and then they go down. My editor at HarperCollins took me to lunch one day in New York. He told me how surprised he and the other people at Harper were that the sales of the book kept increasing. Harper had not really advertised the book. Not a single ad in the *New York Times*. Word of mouth, it's as simple as that. I guess I was just lucky in that I produced this history at a time, 1980, 1981, when all those people who had been influenced by the movements of the sixties and seventies were looking for a new, unorthodox view of American history. I just happened to write it at that moment.

DB *It also got a mention of a different kind in the Hollywood movie* Good Will Hunting. *The book is mentioned by the lead character, played by Matt Damon. What was that about?*

In the movie, Matt Damon is talking to his therapist, played by Robin Williams, looking around at his books, "You want to read a real good history book, read Howard Zinn's *A People's History of the United States*. This book will knock you on your ass." To me it was a very nice thing to be mentioned in a nice film, one I respected. It was very interesting to me that you never in any Hollywood film hear anybody recommend a book. It's as if they don't want people to know that there are books. Come to the movies but don't read books. Do you want to know why the book was mentioned in the film? I can think of two reasons. One is that Matt Damon grew up as a neighbor of ours. My wife and I have known him since he was three years old. His mother, Nancy Carlsson-Paige is a remarkable woman, a friend of ours. So we've known Matt for a very long time. I think his mother gave him *A People's History* to read when he was barely able to hold it in his hands. This kid, now twenty-seven, grew up as a very politically aware kid. This is one explanation. The other explanation is that he was repaying me for the cookies we used to give him when he came around. I was happy and excited to hear the book mentioned like that. I still get phone calls from people all over the country and the first thing they say to me is, Have you seen *Good Will Hunting*?

DB *There are some interesting scenes in the film beyond the mention of your book, a couple of scenes where Will, played by Damon, is laying out his political philosophy, such as when he goes to a job interview for the National Security Agency.*

I don't like to say that there's a scene in the book that's even more important than the mention of *A People's History*, but to me the high point of this film is where this newly discovered working class genius is being sought after by the National Security Agency. They want to give him a job. He's listening to them very skeptically. Then he says, and he does this very quickly, a quick riff through this scenario, it's delightful: Oh, yes. I understand. I'll work at breaking the codes for you. This will enable you to bomb villages in some Third World country to stop a revolution there. But that probably won't work so you'll probably have to send soldiers over there. Some of those soldiers will be my buddies from South Boston. Those of them who survive and come back will find their jobs no longer exist because the company that hired them has moved to the country we just bombed. It was a wonderful little piece, very rare, to find that kind of critique of American foreign policy in a Hollywood movie. I was sorry that when they showed clips for the Academy Awards they didn't show that scene. An oversight, of course.

DB *The Academy Award the film received was for the screenplay.*

That's right. It's a sort of rare thing for two young people together, to get an award for the screenplay, he and Ben Affleck.

DB *Rupert Murdoch's News Corporation owns HarperCollins, the publisher of* A People's History. *It also controls Fox TV and 20th Century Fox. Murdoch's Fox TV network may turn* A People's History *into a miniseries. What light can you shed on this, as the pundits like to ask?*

I could say that Murdoch is repaying me for the cookies I used to give him. But frankly, I'm baffled by it. But it's a possibility. Fox TV seems to be interested in turning *A People's History* into a ten-hour dramatized miniseries. I've been out to Los Angeles twice for meetings with Fox executives and joining me in this enterprise have been Matt Damon and Ben Affleck. The three of us, along with Chris Moore, who was one of the producers of *Good Will Hunting*, are slated to be executive producers of this miniseries. We're in the early stages, and I can't say definitely that it will happen. But it's moving in that direction.

DB *Clearly you recognize that if this project is consummated the potential audience is huge.*

Television is seen by millions of people. If it's well done it will be seen by many millions of people. If it remains true to the point of view of the book, which we will try to ensure, then I would feel that something important has been accomplished. I think it would be a dramatic high point in American culture, without exaggerating the importance of my book, to take any kind of radical view of American society and place it before millions of people, just as Michael Moore did in his work. It's a rare thing in our society.

DB *In some ways, if this TV series sees the light of day, it would also be a payback for you, not just in monetary terms. Throughout your career you have done so many mitzvahs, good deeds, for so many people, talking in front of small groups for no money and traveling to remote places and accumulating all this, the Buddhists would say, good karma. In a way it would be a wonderful kind of capping of all of your work.*

I'm glad you think so. It would be nice to see. Very often people labor and labor but never see the fruits of their labor. So when that does happen we should be happy about that. It would be nice if that took place.

DB *Just talking about a recent mitzvah, you did a benefit talk in Cambridge for Revolution Books, not exactly the Barnes & Noble or Borders of the Boston metropolitan area. You talked about Antonio Gramsci and the importance of culture. Paraphrasing Gramsci, Politics can be controlled but at the cultural level people and ideas can change. Do you believe that?*

Yes, in fact, probably the culture has a better chance of changing than the political structure, because the political structure is very tightly controlled. The economic system is very tightly controlled. In the culture of a society there are more openings and possibilities and in the realm of ideas it is possible for people to begin to think new ideas before they have the opportunity to change their institutions. But if a culture changes enough, if the ideas of people change enough, then beneath the surface of politics and economics there's a bubbling that takes place, an energy that grows and finally breaks through the surface and then you see political and economic institutions change. I think that very often social change takes place in that sequence, the quiet changes beneath the surface and the culture becoming more and more powerful and breaking through.

DB *Another Italian writer you've been quoting and you write about in the* Progressive *article is Ignazio Silone and his novel* Fontamara. *What did you find in* Fontamara *of value?*

First of all Ignazio Silone is one of my heroes, a brilliant novelist under Mussolini's Italy, in exile for a long time, a member of the Communist Party for a while but who left the party in disillusionment, as many people did. He retained his radical humanism. In *Fontamara*, which is a novel about peasants in this little village in Italy under fascism, what struck me was when these peasants were organizing an underground resistance, again talking about changing the culture, before they could overtly resist, create partisan groups, they circulated underground newspapers. They had this newspaper in which they simply reported things that were going on, things that had been done to people. So-and-so has been arrested. This woman has been abused. So-and-so has had land taken away. They would recite these facts, telling people what was going on. Then at the end of it they would simply say, "*che fare?*" What should we do? They wouldn't tell people what to do. They would simply give them the information and suggest by their question that something should be done and leave it to the people to figure out what they could best do. To me that was a marvelous example of how to resist and how to do it in a way that is sensitive to what people can do.

DB *A couple of years ago you spent a few months teaching in Bologna, an Italian city with a left culture, the site of Europe's oldest university. What was that like for you?*

It's always wonderful being in Italy. Bologna is a great city, not just the site of the oldest university. It's often called Red Bologna because it has had Left city leadership for a long time, Communist mayors, and a very powerful working class movement. But also because its buildings are of a kind of red hue, not exactly red, maybe an ochre color, that gives the city a certain kind of glow which matches the politics. It was wonderful being with Italian students and reading the Italian newspaper every day, which I was laboriously doing to try to improve my Italian. It's always good to get out of the U.S., go somewhere else, make contact with other people. If there's hope in the world, a good deal of that hope rests in the intermingling of people all over the world. I have this idea that if people cross enough borders enough times, they're like people stepping on chalk lines again and again. The chalk lines become fainter and fainter. My hope is that national boundaries will become fainter and fainter and we'll get to the point where you won't have visas, passports, border guards, customs officials. I remember you telling me about the terrible atmosphere that accompanies being stopped by customs officials, the helpless feeling you have in the face of overwhelming authority.

DB *With dogs sniffing at your feet.*

Not little fluffy, benign dogs, but those K-9 dogs that threaten you. I look forward to some point in history, whether it comes in my lifetime or later, when people will no longer think of people who live on the other side of a boundary as strangers and often as enemies.

DB   *Are we seeing some ferment in the U.S.? I'm thinking about the very successful and widely supported UPS strike, the defeat of fast track legislation, the derailment of the Multilateral Agreement on Investment, the stopping of the Iraq bombing, and even the victory on organic food labeling.*

Again, going back to the title I gave that chapter, "The Unreported Resistance," yes, there are things that are unreported or underreported or passed over quickly every day that I think are indications of progress being made.

DB   *This is like taking to heart something Marlin Fitzwater once said. He was George Bush's press secretary. You conclude A People's History with this particular incident in 1992: "The Republican Party held a dinner to raise funds at which individuals and corporations paid up to $400,000 to attend. Fitzwater told reporters, 'It's buying access to the system, yes.' When asked about people who didn't have so much money, he replied, 'They have to demand access in other ways.' "*

I hope Fitzwater is honored by my mention of him at the end of my book. I thought that was a very telling statement, that people will have to find access in other ways if they don't have that kind of money. He's giving us good advice, telling us that if we are going to change the system we are going to have to organize, we're going to have to create power, we're going to have to do it without that wealth and without the military force that the government has at its command. I suppose I wanted to end the book with that kind of warning and lesson given by somebody in the Establishment who knows how things happen.

DB   *I think by your work and your spirit of solidarity, your People's History of the United States, that you've done much to provide access to many people. Thanks very much.*

Thank you.

Index

About the Authors

Howard Zinn, professor emeritus at Boston University, is one of this country's most distinguished historians. He was an active figure in the civil rights and anti-Vietnam War movements. His seminal book, *A People's History of the United States*, is widely used in high schools, colleges and universities. His latest book is *Marx in Soho*. In 1998, Howard Zinn was honored with the Lannen Foundation Literary Award and the Eugene V. Debs Award for his writing and political activism.

David Barsamian is founder and director of Alternative Radio. The weekly, award-winning broadcast is a radical departure from the nuzak that prevails in the mainstream media. AR is aired on public and community stations in the U.S., Canada, South Africa and Australia. Barsamian has a series of books with Noam Chomsky; the most recent one is *The Common Good*.

ALTERNATIVE RADIO'S
HOWARD ZINN AUDIO ARCHIVE

All the interviews in this book are available on tape. In addition, here are some other selections from AR's Zinn archive. All programs may be ordered individually. For a complete list of programs, call to request a free catalogue, 1-800-444-1977.

- *Economic Justice*, 10/5/98, $13.
- *Bringing Democracy Alive*, 10/5/98, $13.
- *U.S. Imperialism & the War with Spain*, 6/30/98, $13.
- *Zinn 1998 Trilogy*, $35 (the three tapes above).
- *The Case of Sacco & Vanzetti*, 10/9/97, $13.
- *The Zinn Reader*, 10/8/97, $13.
- *The Cold War & the University*, Howard Zinn & Noam Chomsky, 2/20/97, $13.
- *A People's History of the United States*, 11/20/95, $26 (two tapes).
- *The Use & Abuse of History*, 11/13/93, $13.
- *Emma Goldman: A Dangerous Woman*, 2/24/93, $13.
- *1492–1992: The Legacy of Columbus*, 10/9/91, $13.
- *Just & Unjust Wars*, 3/21/91, $26 (two tapes).
- *On the CIA*, Howard Zinn & Richard Haass Debate, 4/12/90, $13.
- *Second Thoughts on the First Amendment*, 10/25/89, $26 (two tapes).
- *Reform or Revolution*, Howard Zinn & William F. Buckley Debate, 1/11/71, $39 (three tapes).

FUTURE OF HISTORY Special Offer

$175 for the entire package of nineteen tapes, (SAVE $72).

Price includes shipping for the U.S. only. Please add $10 for all other countries. Prepaid orders only. Visa and MasterCard accepted.

Alternative Radio, P.O. Box 551, Boulder, Colorado 80306
1-800-444-1977; ar@orci.com
www.freespeech.org/alternativeradio

marx in soho

"Don't you ever wonder why is it necessary to declare me dead again and again?"

In this witty and insightful "play on history," Howard Zinn brings Karl Marx back to life—literally—to address a contemporary audience. *Marx in Soho* is an invaluable introduction to Marx's life and ideas—and the relevance of Marxism to today's world.

For More Great Books and Information

Award-Winning Common Courage Press has been publishing exposés and authors on the front lines since 1991. Authors include

- Judi Bari
- Peter Breggin
- Joanna Cagan
- Noam Chomsky
- Neil deMause
- Laura Flanders
- Jennifer Harbury

- Margaret Randall
- John Ross
- Ken Silverstein
- Norman Solomon
- Cornel West
- Howard Zinn
- and many others

Also available: the dynamite **The Real Stories Series** of small books from **Odonian Press** including titles from Noam Chomsky and Gore Vidal.

FOR BULK DISCOUNTS CALL 800-497-3207

For catalogs and updates, call 800-497-3207.
Email us at **orders-info@commoncouragepress.com**.
Write us at
Common Courage Press
Box 702
Monroe, ME 04951
Or visit our website at **www.commoncouragepress.com**.

CALL FOR MANUSCRIPTS

We are always looking for new manuscripts and ideas for books. Please don't hesitate to put us in touch with potential authors, or to give us ideas for books you'd like to read.